STARTUP GUIDE
#startupeverywhere

Startup Guide Kigali

EDITORIAL
Publisher: **Sissel Hansen**
Editor: **Hazel Boydell**
Proofreaders: **Ted Hermann, Michelle Mills Smith**

PRODUCTION
Global Production Lead: **Eglė Duleckytė**
Local Production Manager: **Rita Gomes**
Community Managers: **Jiske van Straaten, Daphne Frühmann, Hannah Müller**
Research by **Hannah Müller**

DESIGN & PHOTOGRAPHY
Designer: **Daniela Castanheira**
Illustrations by **Daniela Castanheira, Joana Carvalho, Cat Serafim**
Photo Editors: **Daniela Castanheira, Joana Carvalho**

LOCAL RESEARCH AND DATA
Directory: **Aline Joyce**

PARTNERSHIPS
COO: **Anna Weissensteiner**
anna@startupguide.com

Printed in Berlin, Germany by
Medialis-Offsetdruck GmbH
Heidelbergerstraße 65, 12435 Berlin

Published by **Startup Guide World ApS**
Borgbjergsvej 1, 2450 Copenhagen

info@startupguide.com

Worldwide distribution by **Die Gestalten**
Visit: **gestalten.com**

Visit: **startupguide.com**

ISBN: 978-3-947624-34-8

WRITERS
Alexandra Connerty: SAP Africa Expert P. 88 / Segal Family Foundation P. 94 / Root Capital P. 152 /
Cayleigh Bright: Awesomity Lab P. 32 / Charis UAS P. 38 / Exuus P. 40 / Imagine WE P. 42 / My Green Home P. 46 / 250STARTUPS P. 52 / Challenges Rwanda P. 56 / Resonate P. 66 / FabLab Rwanda P. 70 / Waka P. 78 / Westerwelle Startup Haus Space P. 82 / Henri Nyakarundi P. 118 / University of Rwanda P. 144 / Rwanda Innovation Fund (RIF) P. 156 / Urumuri Program by Bank of Kigali P. 158 /
Kevin Hanley: BeneFactors P. 36 / BPN Rwanda P. 54 / Patrick Buchana Nsenga P. 126 / Rwanda Green Fund (FONERWA) P. 154 /
Kirsty Henderson: Essentials P. 17-29 /
L. Isaac Simon: Christelle Kwizera P. 102 / Clarisse Iribagiza P. 110 /
Phineas Rueckert: Overview of the Ecosystem P. 14 / Kasha P. 44 / African Management Institute P. 138 / Access to Finance P. 148 / East Africa Investments P. 150 /
Tom Jackson: BAG Innovation P. 34 / Rwanda Biosolutions P. 48 / DOT Rwanda P. 58 / G5 Business Makers Program P. 60 / Inkomoko P. 64 / Hanga Ahazaza Program P. 62 / Impact Hub Kigali P. 74 / Klab P. 76 / African Institute for Mathematical Sciences P. 136 / Akilah Institute P. 140 / Moringa School P. 142

PHOTOGRAPHER
Alex Niragira P. 10 / P. 33 / P. 47 / P. 71-73 / P. 75 / P. 83-85 / P. 94,96 / P. 144 / P. 150 / P. 154

ADDITIONAL PHOTOGRAPHY
BAG Innovation P. 35 / Simon Skipper P. 37 /
Charis UAS Ltd P. 39 / Exuus Ltd P. 41 / Joel Gisagara (Dominique portrait) P. 43 / Kasha Global P. 45 /
Rwanda Biosolution Lda P. 49 / 250STARTUPS P. 52 /
Roar Visuals for BPN P. 54 / Misc for Challenges Group P. 56 /
DOT Rwanda P. 58 / Envision Photography P. 60 /
Inkomoko Entrepreneur Development P. 64 /
Illume Creative Studio P. 62 / Resonate P. 66 / Klab P. 76 /
Guez Show for Waka Fitness Ltd P. 79 /
Peter Irungu P. 88 / Christelle Kwizera (Water Access Rwanda) P. 103, 106, 109 /
Clarisse Iribagiza (DMM.HeHe Ltd) P. 111, 114, 117 /
illume for ARED Group LTD - Henri Nyakarundi P. 119, 122, 125 /
AC Group Ltd - Patrick Buchana Nsenga (AC Group) P. 127, 130, 133 /
AIMS (African Institute for Mathematical Sciences) P. 136 /
African Management Institute P. 138 / Davis College P. 140 /
Moringa School P. 142 / Access to Finance P. 148 /
Patricia Alvarado - Grazioso Pictures Inc. P. 152 /
Yael Amir P. 154 / Igihe Ltd P. 158 and One Zone Studio P. 6, 16 /
Simbi Yvan P. 19 / Jannik Skorna P. 20, 26 / Maxime Niyomwungeri P. 22 /
Michael Muli P. 24, 28 / Alvin Engler P. 90-91 from Unsplash.com

---

Copyright © 2020 Startup Guide World ApS All rights reserved.

Although the authors and publisher have made every effort to ensure that the information in this book is correct, they do not assume and hereby disclaim any liability to any party for any loss, damage, or disruption caused by errors or omissions, whether such errors or omissions result from negligence, accident, or any other cause. No part of this publication may be reproduced, distributed, or transmitted in any form or by any means, including photocopying, recording, or other electronic or mechanical methods, without the prior written permission of the publisher, except in the case of brief quotations embodied in critical reviews and certain other non-commercial uses permitted by copyright law.

onetreeplanted.org

STARTUP GUIDE
KIGALI

STARTUP GUIDE KIGALI

In partnership with
Westerwelle Startup Haus Kigali

Proudly supported by

SAP

german cooperation
DEUTSCHE ZUSAMMENARBEIT

giz Deutsche Gesellschaft
für Internationale
Zusammenarbeit (GIZ) GmbH

Make-IT in Africa
inspire. connect. develop.

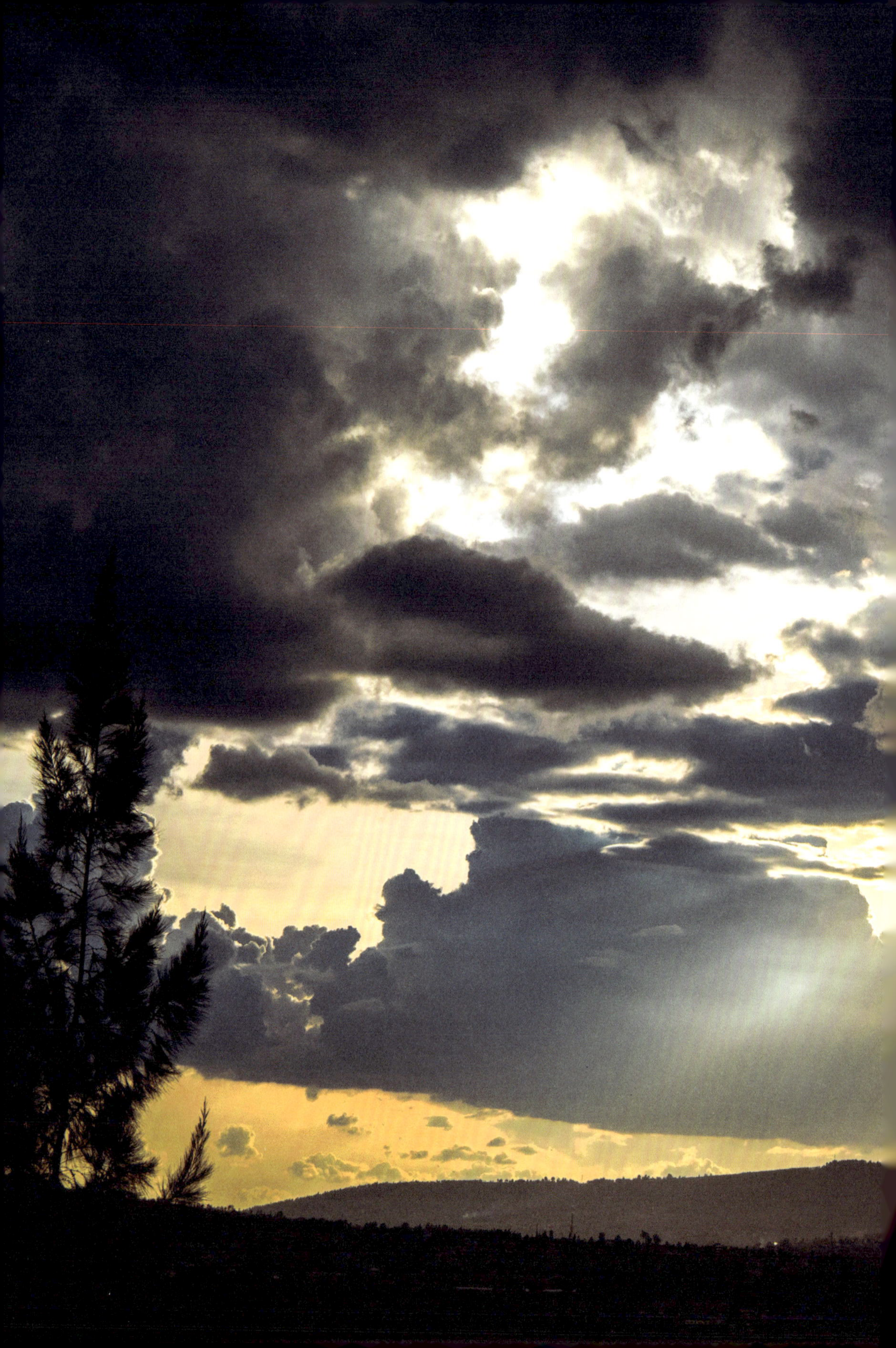

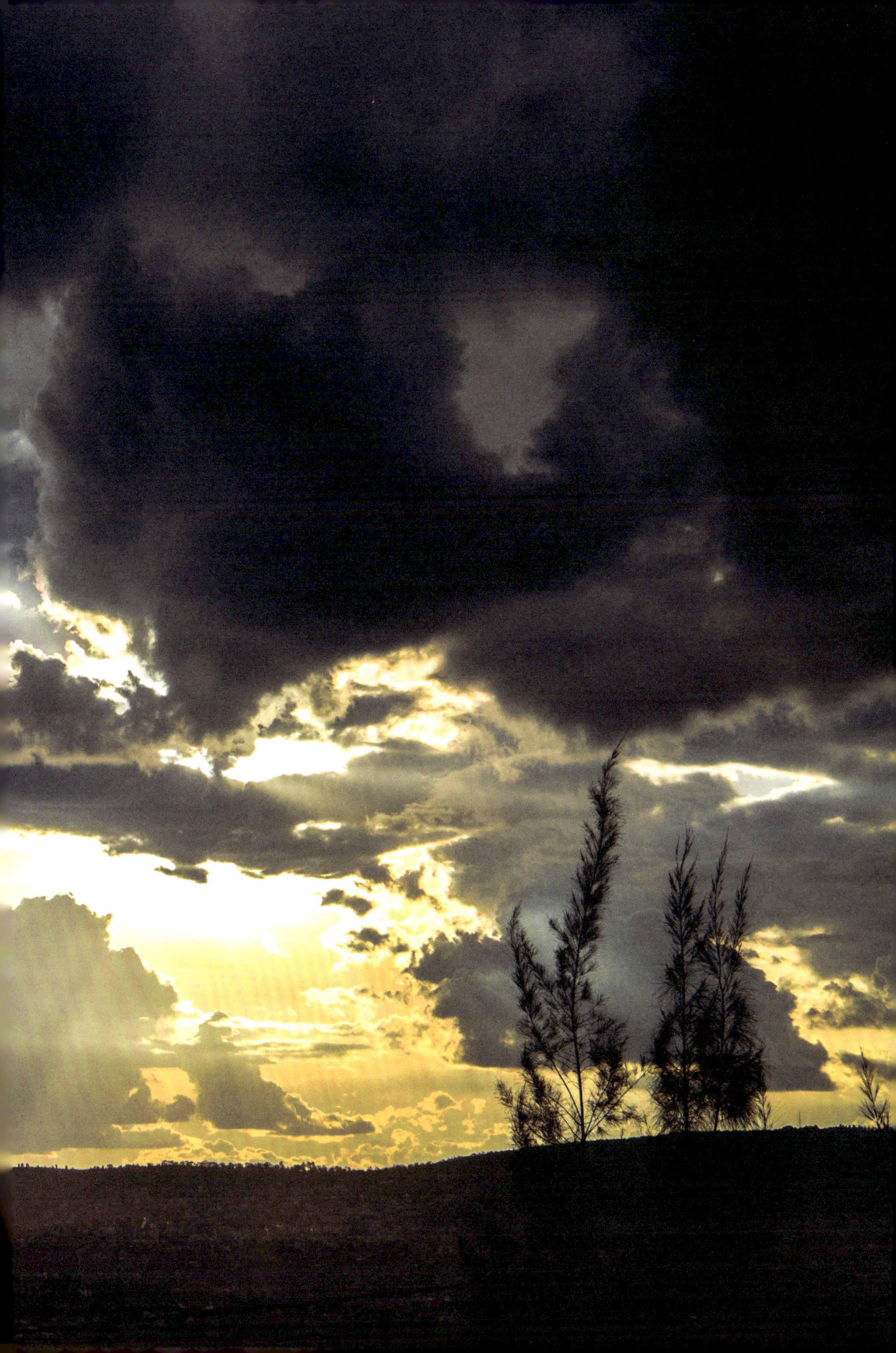

introduction

Sissel Hansen
/ Startup Guide

Rwanda is a small country, but by thinking bigger than its borders, it's quickly becoming an important African tech hub. In recent years, its government has invested heavily in infrastructure and business development, such as the creation of Kigali Innovation City. Kigali is also a popular location for events and conferences, including Africa Tech Summit, which creates links with other continental and global business communities. This collaborative African business network is part of what inspired us to launch the Africa impact series, which is made possible by our partnership with SAP. *Startup Guide Kigali* comes alongside titles dedicated to purpose-driven initiatives in Nairobi, Accra and Lagos. Together, we hope they shine a light on the continent's startup ecosystems.

With a dedicated entrepreneur visa, a quick and easy business registration process and a high level of both English and French, it's clear to see why Kigali is an attractive option for international entrepreneurs. Rwanda was the second-highest-rated African country in the World Bank's *Doing Business 2020* report, after Mauritius. But Kigali is more than a great place to start a business. It's a safe, green and lively city spread across hills and valleys, and it's also ahead of the crowd in some environmental and social initiatives – plastic bags have been banned for years, and the whole country participates in the community-building initiative *umuganda* each month.

Kigali has high-quality startup hubs such as our community partner Westerwelle Startup Haus Kigali, as well as excellent accelerators and programs driving innovation. Westerwelle Startup Haus Kigali was hugely helpful in connecting us with the local ecosystem, and we quickly learned that the city's entrepreneurs are passionate, inspired and have a strong collective desire to solve the world's most pressing problems. Pioneering agritech companies such as Rwanda Biosolution are rethinking Africa's farming industry, and fintech firm Exuus uses blockchain to revolutionize savings groups and help low-income communities become more financially resilient. Across the board, you'll see local entrepreneurs using technology to improve their communities and contribute on a global scale.

It's clear that Kigali's tech scene has huge potential for growth and that its startup ecosystem is quickly evolving. We'll be sure to keep an eye on how it develops, but for now we're excited to share the stories of the city's most impactful startups and hope that they inspire you.

Sissel Hansen
Founder and CEO of Startup Guide

Kigali

Local Community Partner / Westerwelle Startup Haus Kigali

Welcome to Kigali, the cleanest and safest city in Africa.

Kigali is home to roughly 1.29 million inhabitants, of which 60 percent is youth. Strategically located at the heart of the continent, Kigali is the second-largest destination for meetings, events and conferences (MICE) in Africa and therefore a major meeting point for governments, investors and corporations from all over the continent. Kigali is the main economic, cultural and financial hub of Rwanda, serving as the country's main point of entry and business center.

The startup scene in Kigali is one of the fastest-growing on the continent, with a favorable regulatory framework, a young and innovative population, world-class higher learning institutions, avant-garde environmental policies and entirely digitalized government services. It's been a privilege to witness the evolution of this ecosystem over the last ten years. From medical supplies delivered by drones to new recycling techniques in construction, innovations from Kigali continue to attract entrepreneurs and investors willing to leave a long-lasting impact.

Westerwelle Startup Haus Kigali (WSHK) has become a significant player in this ecosystem. Beyond our coworking space and maker space, WSHK is considered an entry point for investors, entrepreneurial support organizations and new actors coming to Kigali. Our entrepreneurship program provides support to early-stage startups by providing tailor-made workshops, mentorship and advisory services in a variety of sectors. Furthermore, WSHK is known for its conveniently central location next to the Kigali Convention Centre, its multicultural community and its unique networking events.

Startup Guide Kigali offers a unique experience of Kigali, highlighting the resources you need to discover the city. I wish you success in your future projects here and will be more than happy to welcome you to Westerwelle Startup Haus Kigali.

All the best,

Sangwa Rwabuhihi
General Manager / Westerwelle Startup Haus Kigali

contents

Startup Guide Kigali

overview 14 essentials 16 directory 160 glossary 164 about the guide 166

startups

Awesomity Lab **32**
BAG Innovation **34**
BeneFactors **36**
Charis UAS **38**
Exuus **40**
Imagine We **42**
Kasha **44**
My Green Home **46**
Rwanda Biosolution **48**

programs

250STARTUPS **52**
BPN Rwanda **54**
Challenges Rwanda **56**
Digital Opportunity Trust Rwanda **58**
G5 Business Makers Program **60**
Hanga Ahazaza **62**
Inkomoko Entrepreneur Development **64**
Resonate **66**

spaces

FabLab Rwanda **70**
Impact Hub Kigali **74**
kLab **76**
WAKA **78**
Westerwelle Startup Haus Kigali **82**

experts

In Partnership With:
SAP **88**
Segal Family Foundation **94**

founders

Christelle Kwizera / Water Access Rwanda **102**
Clarisse Iribagiza / DMM.HeHe **110**
Henri Nyakarundi / ARED **118**
Patrick Buchana Nsenga / AC Group **126**

schools

African Institute for Mathematical Sciences **136**
African Management Institute **138**
Akilah Institute **140**
Moringa School **142**
University of Rwanda **144**

investors

Access to Finance Rwanda **148**
East Africa Investments **150**
Root Capital **152**
Rwanda Green Fund (FONERWA) **154**
Rwanda Innovation Fund **156**
Urumuri by Bank of Kigali **158**

overview

Local Ecosystem

[Facts & Figures]
- Kigali was ranked the 226th-best startup ecosystem in the world in 2020, six places higher than the year before.
- Kigali Innovation City, a $2 billion government-led project to build a base for entrepreneurs in Rwanda, will create 50,000 construction jobs and aims to bring in $300 million in foreign direct investment.
- According to the 2020 Global Gender Gap Index, Rwanda ranks ninth in the world in gender equality – the only African country in the top ten. Women represent 43.2% of entrepreneurs in Kigali.
- Every two years, Kigali hosts the Transform Africa conference, a tech event aimed at developing ICT tech leaders across Africa with representatives from more than a dozen countries.
- Kigali is second only to Cape Town in the number of international conferences hosted in an African city.
- Kigali uses the Rwandan franc (FRw). The average exchange rate over the twelve months before publication was FRw 1 = $0.00106531051.

[Notable Startups]
- AC Group developed a cashless app for bus travel that has been adopted in cities around the region.
- Charis UAS, Rwanda's first certified unmanned aircraft system (UAS) company, uses drone technology to identify mosquito breeding sites and apply targeted insecticide in the fight against malaria.
- BAG Innovation was one of eleven startups selected for the 2020 Pitch Live at Africa Startup Summit.

Sources: *Startup Ecosystems Ranking Report 2020* (Startup Blink), "Rwanda is Building Africa's Very Own Silicon Valley – Known as Kigali Innovation City (KIC)" (semiwiki.com), *2020 Global Gender Gap Index* (World Economic Forum), *The Sustainability of Businesses in Kigali, Rwanda: An Analysis of the Barriers Faced by Women Entrepreneurs, Startup Report: 2017 Emerging Startups* (iD&D Ltd.), "Kigali, smart city and hub of digital transformation in Africa" (tactis.fr), "Could cashless payments make Rwanda's bus conductor redundant?" (bbc.com), "Rwanda: Use of Drones in Malaria Fight to Begin With Gasabo" (allafrica.com), baginnovation.rw, populationstat.com, "No slums and a 'vision city': an impression of Kigali's housing" (urbantransformations.ox.ac.uk), worldbank.org, xe.com

[City] # Kigali, Rwanda

[Statistics]
Urban population: 745,261
Metropolitan population: 1,129,742
Area: 730 km²
Population density: 1,552 per km²
GDP (Rwanda): $1.5 billion

STARTUP GUIDE KIGALI

essentials

Grand Pension Plaza - Kigali, Rwanda

essentials

Intro to the City

Rwanda is often touted as one of Africa's shining stars of development and, after living through some very dark days, this small country is definitely on the rise. It's remarkably easy to start a business here, and its capital city, Kigali, is full of opportunity and excitement for the future.

It is a tiny nation of twelve million people, but Rwanda's location right next to the Democratic Republic of Congo and its membership in the East African Community – which has a population of over 150 million – means that it's in the middle of a region with tremendous opportunity. The country routinely ranks as one of the least corrupt in Africa and its forward-thinking government is constantly pushing towards ambitious development goals, actively supporting business owners along the way.

Kigali is a stunning, green city set across several hills and offering perfect weather. It's small enough to get around easily, but large enough to keep things interesting. It's also one of the safest and cleanest capitals in the world. Rwandans are warm and friendly and newcomers will find Kigali an easy place to find their feet. It might not be as freewheeling as some other African cities, but Kigali has a charm all its own with a slow, calm pace and a feeling that the country is collectively moving toward something great.

Before You Come 18

Visas and Work Permits 18

Cultural Differences 21

Cost of Living 21

Accommodation 23

Insurance 23

Taxes 25

Starting a Company 25

Opening a Bank Account 27

Getting Around 27

Phone and Internet 27

Learning the Language 29

Meeting People 29

Before You Come

Kigali can be a very affordable place to live, but make sure you have savings for initial expenses. It's recommended that you arrange to rent a room in a shared house while you search for a more permanent place. Check out **airbnb.com** or the Facebook groups **Expats in Rwanda** and **Living in Kigali** for leads. Pick up a map from **mapofkigali.com** before arriving as it's the most accurate map of the city and packed with information useful for newcomers. A yellow fever vaccine is required and you'll need it for international travel within the region. Malaria is more common in the countryside than in Kigali and many foreigners choose to forgo antimalarial medication, but check with your doctor for advice on this and other vaccines.
All residence permits require a police certificate from your country of residence for the previous six months and some visas require notarized copies of academic certificates, so be sure to bring these.

Visas and Work Permits

Rwanda prides itself on its openness and offers a progressive and forward-thinking visa program. Citizens from every nation in the world are entitled to a thirty-day visa on arrival, which is free for citizens of the African Union, Commonwealth and Francophonie member states. Visa rules change often, so check **irembo.gov.rw** for the latest information and to start your application for either a temporary or permanent residence permit. Most foreigners apply for a temporary permit, of which there are over twenty categories. If you want to travel among Rwanda, Uganda and Kenya, the East African Tourist Visa is an excellent option, but it doesn't allow you to work.

You can find a full list of visas, the documents required for each and printable application forms at **migration.gov.rw**. The application process can be started overseas but must be completed at the Rwanda Immigration and Emigration office in Kigali within fifteen days of your arrival. Bring proof of payment, your passport and the required documents and get to the office just before it opens at 7 AM to avoid a long wait. You'll also be required to get a residency card at the same office. Visas range in price but both business and employment visas cost FRw 150,000 ($160) and are usually issued for two years (depending on the whims of the immigration officer). Government guidelines say that it takes two days to issue visas but two weeks is more common.

See **Important Government Offices** page **162**

essentials

Kigali City Tower - Kigali, Rwanda

essentials

Kimisagara Football for Hope Centre - Kigali, Rwanda

Cultural Differences

There is a general sense of hope, solidarity and positivity about the future in Rwanda, but recognition of its tragic history can't be ignored. Never raise the topic of the genocide against the Tutsi or ask about anyone's ethnicity – as a policy, everyone is now Rwandan. Talking about politics, especially in public, is frowned upon and doing so might make people around you uncomfortable. To foster community, neighbors gather together for *umuganda* on the last Saturday of each month to work on local projects. As a foreigner you're exempt from umuganda (but welcome to participate) and you shouldn't leave your house until after work is completed at 11 AM on these days. Rwandan society as a whole is conservative, though Kigali a little less so. People dress modestly and are generally polite and non-confrontational. It can take some time to really get to know Rwandans, but if you make an effort you're sure to create some solid new friendships.

Cost of Living

Kigali can offer a very nice standard of living on a monthly budget of FRw 1 million to FRw 1.5 million ($1,065–$1,600). This is plenty for a room in a modern shared house, groceries including imported items, daily transport on motorcycle taxis, gym membership and nights out. A meal and a beer at a local pub can be as low as FRw 5,000 (around $5) but you will pay closer to FRw 20,000 ($19) at a nice restaurant. Monthly membership at a modern gym such as WAKA Fitness starts at around FRw 28,000 ($30) and a 30 GB pay-as-you-go data package is around FRw 9,400 ($10) per month. Private schools range from approx FRw 6.6 million ($7,000) for high school at Green Hills to over FRw 18 million (around $19,000) for the International School of Kigali annually. Buying a car can be expensive and gas usually hovers around FRw 1,000 (just over $1) per liter. The cost of living in Kigali, as anywhere, will depend on your quality of life, but it's easy to live well here for less than in many other parts of the world.

essentials

Sunrise - Kigali, Rwanda

Accommodation

Most people live in houses rather than apartments in Kigali. Facebook groups, including **Expats in Rwanda** and **Living in Kigali**, are great places to start your search for a room in a shared house. Renting a whole house is trickier, but there are property agents to help. Always get personal recommendations before choosing an agent and note that they'll usually charge a finder's fee equal to your first month's rent. Renting a room is often informal and done without a tenancy agreement, but if you're renting a house make sure to get everything in writing. Generally, you can find a nice room for around FRw 375,000 ($400) per month and a house for an average of about FRw 1 million ($1,065). Foreigners are expected to hire help – usually a guard (or a security agency) and a cleaner at a minimum. This can feel strange, but it's a part of the culture. Churches here can be very loud, so take this into consideration when choosing where to live.

See **Accommodation** page **161**

Insurance

Health insurance isn't mandatory in Rwanda and many foreigners staying for shorter stays will take out travel insurance and call it a day. For those who want more extensive coverage or who are staying for longer, taking out a local policy is a good idea. UAP is a popular choice among foreigners – the company offers every type of insurance policy you could think of, including individual and family medical coverage and vehicle and liability insurance. You can get a quote at uap-group.com. Outpatient services in Rwanda are very affordable, which is worth keeping in mind when choosing a plan. No local health insurance provider will offer repatriation of a body, though many will fly you to Kenya or South Africa for treatment of serious injuries and illness. Those coming to Rwanda as employees should negotiate health insurance coverage with their employer. Car insurance is mandatory here but home and business insurance are less commonly used.

See **Insurance Companies** page **163**

essentials

Inema Arts Centre - Kigali, Rwanda

Taxes

Taxes are collected quarterly by the Rwandan Revenue Authority (RRA). The online filing system is fairly straightforward, but fines for missing deadlines are harsh. Accountants are affordable and hiring a firm is recommended. Businesses that earn under FRw 20,000,000 ($21,300) annually can choose to file taxes using the lump sum regime, under which they're taxed 3 percent and have no requirement to file expenses. Businesses that earn more must use the real regime, under which expenses are accounted for and a tax of 30 percent is levied on net earnings. A value-added tax (VAT) of 18 percent is charged on most goods and services. If your business nets over FRw 200,000,000 ($213,000) annually, you're required to collect VAT and pay this quarterly to RRA (but you can claim VAT on your business-related expenses). There are various other taxes depending on your circumstances, so consult the RRA website at rra.gov.rw.

See **Financial Services** page **162**

Starting a Company

Registering a business in Rwanda is incredibly simple and the government prides itself on its openness to commerce. As a foreigner you can register a business on arrival for free and be up and running within twenty-four hours. Just go to the Rwanda Development Board with a business concept and name, fill in a few forms (there are people there to help you through the process), and you'll be issued a Certificate of Domestic Company Registration and tax number (TIN) the same day. You will need to include your TIN on all of your invoices. Rwandans love official stamps so get one made with your business name, TIN and phone number (it's a cheap and easy process at a stationary shop). Once you have these things, you're ready to start trading – it's as simple as that.

To get a business visa, you'll need your registration certificate and an immigration official will want to visit your place of business, so you'll need to rent an office, even if it's only temporary. Additionally, you're required to have a trading license (also known as *patente*), which costs between FRw 40,000 (around $43) and FRw 90,000 ($96) depending on the turnover of the business and must be paid annually.

See **Programs** page **50**

essentials

Mountain view - Kigali, Rwanda

Opening a Bank Account

Opening a personal bank account in Rwanda is simple once you have a residency permit of any kind. Just choose a bank (Access, Ecobank and Bank of Kigali are popular and have good internet banking) and take your passport and a passport-sized photo. For a business account, you will also need a business certificate. Some, but not all, banks offer POS machines, so if this is important to you, make sure to check. Banks here generally offer good customer service, and staff members will often give you their contact details and are responsive when you need help. You can use local and international cards in any ATM across the city and some have an option of dispensing US dollars. The fee for international withdrawals is usually around FRw 2,000 ($2). Kigali is still largely a cash city, but it's possible to use local and foreign bank and credit cards in a growing number of shops and restaurants.

See **Banks** page **161**

Getting Around

Motorcycle taxis (motos) are Kigali's most popular form of transport and you'll see them everywhere. They are strictly one passenger per bike and the driver will provide a helmet. The minimum fare is FRw 300 ($0.32), and you'll rarely pay more than FRw 1,200 (about $1.30) for a ride. Car taxis are far more expensive and difficult to flag down. You can use apps like Yego and VW Move to book a taxi, but most people have a collection of contact details for individual taxi drivers. Kigali has an excellent bus network that runs across the city, with destinations clearly displayed at the front of the bus. Fares are based on distance but are usually under FRw 500 ($0.50) per ride. To use the bus, you'll need a Tap&Go card, which can be topped up at some stops and all stations. Traffic in Kigali is bearable, but things can still get busy during rush hour.

Phone and Internet

The two main telecom companies in Rwanda are MTN and Airtel. You can pick up a SIM card for around FRw 1,000 ($1) at their branch offices and you'll need a copy of your passport to register, even for pay-as-you-go. A 30 GB pay-as-you-go data package costs around FRw 10,000 (around $10) per month, and minutes are cheap. Wireless internet in Rwanda can be temperamental and people often choose their phone provider based on which one has the best signal at their home. Internet coverage is patchy in certain parts of the city and consistent 4G is still a rarity. MTN has a mobile money app, MoMo, that is growing in popularity and is incredibly useful, especially for paying bills. Liquid Telecom is recommended for fiber optic but it's not available everywhere yet. For fast, reliable and free internet many people work from the Marriott Hotel.

essentials

28

Inema Arts Centre - Kigali, Rwanda

Learning the Language

The national language of Rwanda is Kinyarwanda but English is widely spoken in Kigali and is the language of choice for commerce and government. In 2010, Rwanda switched the language of instruction in schools from French to English so younger people are likely to speak English and it's more common for older Rwandans to know French (though many Kigalians are trilingual). Outside of Kigali, people are more likely to speak only Kinyarwanda. If you want to learn Kinyarwanda, you're in for a fun ride; as a Bantu language it's quite different from European languages and learning can feel like a puzzle to native English speakers. **Inzora Rooftop Café** runs regular introductory group classes and finding a private tutor is easy and affordable. Google Translate features Kinyarwanda, which can also help you learn a little. Rwandans will light up when they hear you speak their language and that alone is worth making the effort, even if it's just for a few common phrases.

See **Language Schools** page **163**

Meeting People

Meeting people in Kigali is quite easy, especially if you're outgoing and have a wide variety of interests. One of the quickest ways to meet friends is to move into a shared house. There's also a Facebook group for every activity you could think of, so look around and you're sure to find your tribe. Keep an eye out for events at major hotels and at coworking spaces like **Impact Hub**. Another option is to join the **Hash House Harriers**, a global running group with an active chapter in Kigali. The foreign community in Kigali is warm and welcoming, and you can usually find plenty of other recent arrivals eager to explore. Rwandans can be reserved, but if you attend church, get involved in neighborhood activities or work in a local company you'll find that many are eager to get to know you.

See **Groups and Meetups** page **162** and **Startup Events** page **163**

start

ups

Awesomity Lab **32**

BAG Innovation **34**

BeneFactors **36**

Charis UAS **38**

Exuus **40**

Imagine We **42**

Kasha **44**

My Green Home **46**

Rwanda Biosolution **48**

startups

Awesomity Lab

[Name]

[Elevator Pitch] *"We are a software-development company that focuses on user-centered design to create the greatest possible impact for our clients. At our core, we are a team of designers, engineers and creatives who came together to create world-class software solutions."*

[The Story] Awesomity Lab's CEO and chairman Lionel Mpfizi met his cofounders at a six-month tech boot camp held by HeHe Labs (now DMM.HeHe). From their college library, the four friends became a team, growing in skills and learning on the go. "The unique thing about Awesomity, and, I believe, one of the reasons businesses choose to work with us, is our approach to work," says Lionel. "We spent a lot of time in trial and error, trying to figure out the best ways to approach problem solving, design and so on."

Now a team of fifteen full-time employees and six interns, the company builds mobile applications and web platforms with a focus on user-centered design. It counts Volkswagen among its clients and has created over two hundred websites for various departments of the Rwandan government. "We took risks by taking on huge projects and had a lot of learnings from them. It all led to us crafting the perfect process to work with businesses, where we don't just offer technology solutions, but offer solutions that will have an impact in the businesses we're working with," Lionel says. The company was awarded the Rwanda Tech Seal for Best Practices in Programming and received the Young Entrepreneur of the Year award at the 2019 RDB Business Excellence Awards.

[Funding History]

Bootstrap

Awesomity Lab's founders decided to bootstrap the company after a few failed attempts at raising seed money. The company has been profitable since 2018 and is seeking opportunities to expand to other African locations.

[Milestones]
- Meeting at a six-month coding program and deciding to collaborate as cofounders.
- Taking the first runner-up position in Seedstars Kigali 2016, which motivated us greatly.
- Winning a contract to create the VW Move app for Volkswagen.
- Winning the Gov UX challenge, allowing us to redesign Rwandan government-owned websites.

[Links] Web: awesomity.rw LinkedIn: company/awesomitylab Facebook: awesomitylab
Instagram: awesomitylab Twitter: @awesomitylab

Awesomity Lab

startups

[Name] # BAG Innovation

[Elevator Pitch] *"We combine AI and gamification to revolutionize the future of career guidance. Our platform simulates virtual market challenges and provides feedback and advice to students throughout their university journey."*

[The Story] Founded in 2017, BAG Innovation is a digital support system that helps university students acquire market-relevant experience and exposure. With curricula struggling to keep up with the evolving marketplace and career centers not always serving students as they should, the startup uses a combination of AI and gamification to simulate virtual challenges posed by organizations. Students submit solutions and receive feedback from both the employer and BAG's AI-driven career-development tool. "This results in BAG delivering highly relevant experience-based learning throughout the whole student journey," says cofounder Yussouf Ntwali.

In its early days, BAG sustained its operations by charging for offline talent placement. It has since built out its tech and is now partnered with the majority of Rwanda's universities. More than eight thousand students have used the platform. "BAG Innovation has increased the market readiness score of students by between thirty and sixty percent," says Gabriel Ekman, the startup's managing director. The company has also partnered with the creators of Candy Crush to build its gamification API and further improve the user experience. Gabriel says that "Kigali is becoming a hub for the edtech ecosystem in East Africa and is focusing much effort on supporting the growing tech startups in the country."

[Funding History]

Bootstrap   Pre-Seed   Seed

BAG was bootstrapped before receiving $150,000 in seed funding to scale its technology in 2019.

[Milestones]
- Launching our MVP in mid-2019.
- Securing an MOU with the largest university in Rwanda to roll out BAG on all of the major campuses in the country.
- Celebrating over five hundred users being placed into jobs by 2020.
- Representing the Rwandan edtech scene at the EdTechX summit in 2019 and taking part in the global Seedstars Summit in 2020.

[Links] Web: baginnovation.rw LinkedIn: company/baginnovation. Facebook: BAGInnovationRwanda Instagram: @baginnovation Twitter: @BAG_Innovation

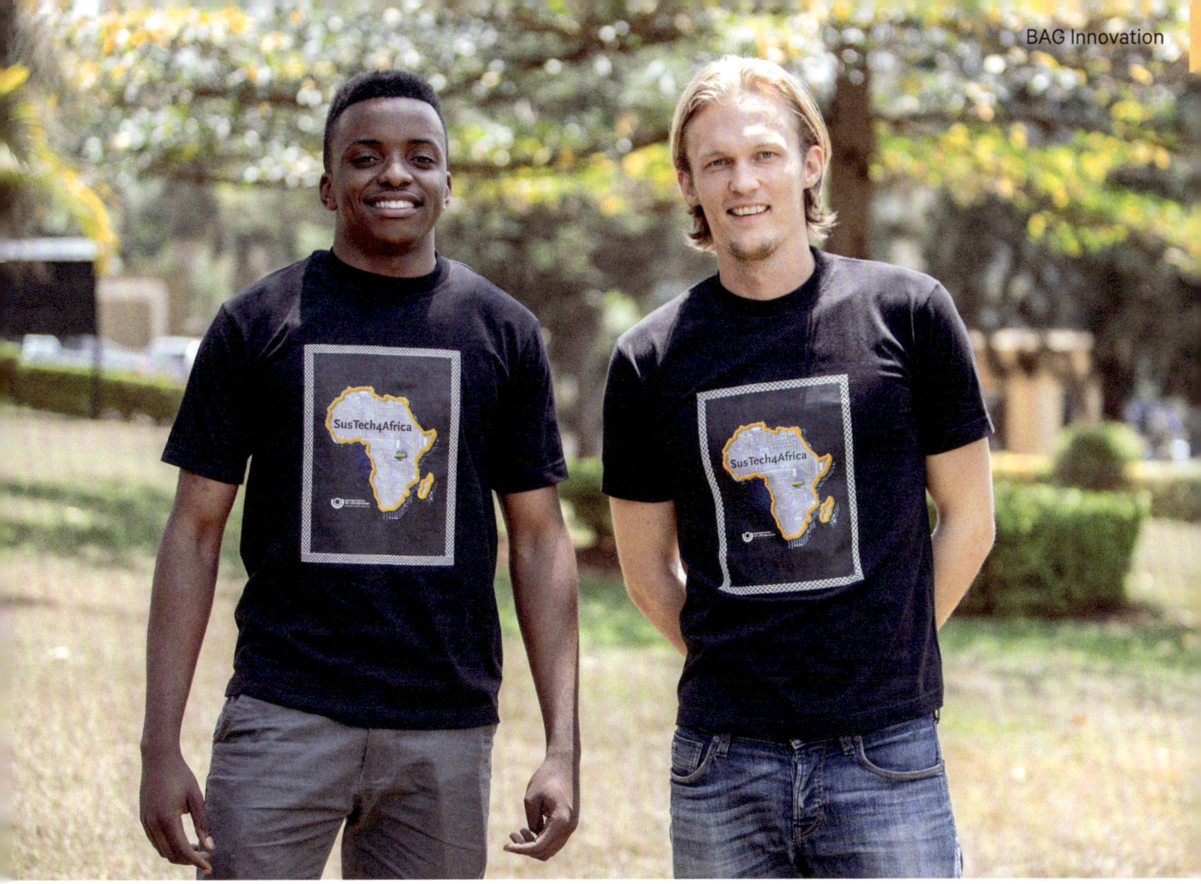
SusTech4Africa
SusTech4Africa

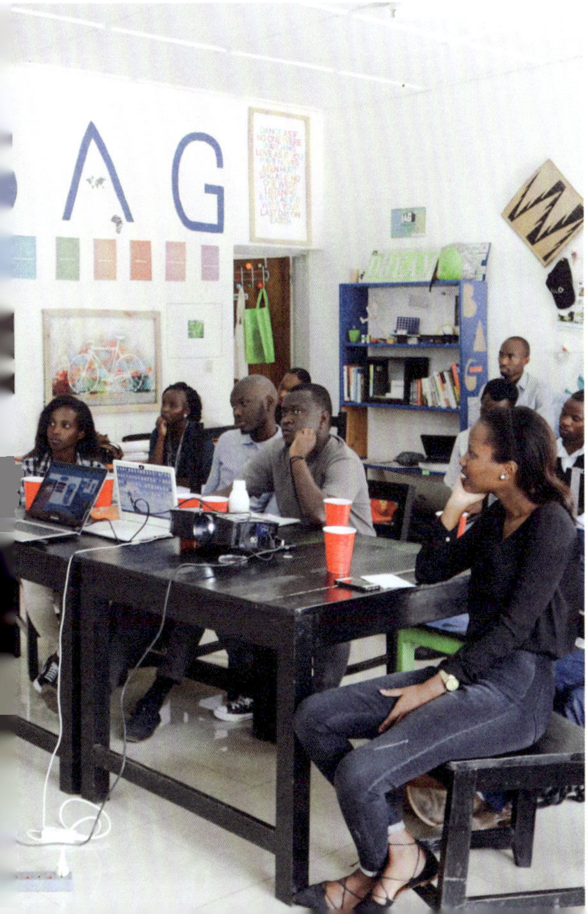
AG

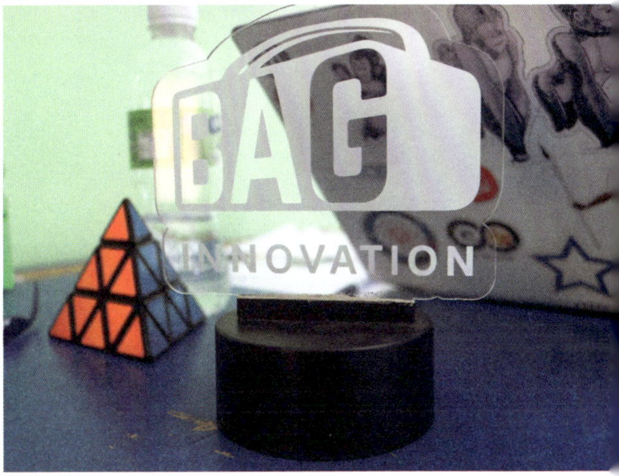
BAG
INNOVATION

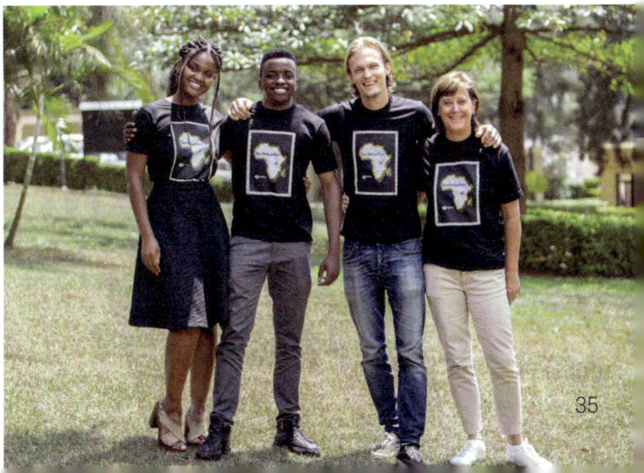

startups

[Name] # BeneFactors

[Elevator Pitch] *"BeneFactors is a factoring company that provides working capital solutions to SMEs across all sectors of the Rwandan economy."*

[The Story] Olivia Zank, the founder and CEO of BeneFactors, started out as an advisor in the Rwandan Ministry of Trade. She was responsible for promoting the exports of small and medium-sized enterprises, but soon noticed that access to capital was the biggest problem that Rwandan SMEs faced. Too big for microfinancing and too small for commercial bank lending, these companies were often left without the financial means to deliver on their promised exports. The ministry worked with banks to convince them to lend to SMEs, but its efforts largely failed. Frustrated, Olivia founded BeneFactors and set up office in the basement of a hotel.

BeneFactors provides factoring services to firms in "the missing middle." Factoring is when a seller hands over their invoices to a third party. The third party pays the invoice and collects payment from the original buyer when it's due. "We're a company that was founded to provide short-term working capital to financially excluded SMEs," Olivia says. Six hundred percent growth in both 2018 and 2019 demonstrates that it was a forward-thinking idea. Now with a team of eleven and handling $750,000 in assets, the company has moved out of that original basement office and has ambitions to expand into other countries.

[Funding History]

Bootstrap   Pre-Seed   Seed

BeneFactors was self-financed before receiving loans from friends and family. It closed a pre-seed round of $190,000 in 2018 and raised $850,000 in debt capital in August 2019, largely through the credit line of a local bank.

[Milestones]
- Hiring the first staff members and settling the first invoices in October 2017.
- Closing the pre-seed round and raising $190,000 in 2018.
- Moving from a hotel basement to an actual office.
- Closing a debt round in August 2019.

[Links] Web: benefactors.io LinkedIn: company/benefactors-ltd Facebook: benefactorsltd
Twitter: @benefactorsltd

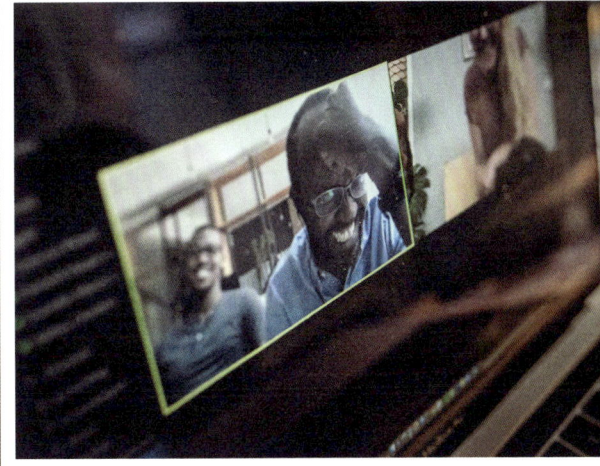

BeneFactors

startups

[Name] # Charis UAS

[Elevator Pitch] *"Charis UAS provides drone imagery and advanced analytics for intelligent decision making to businesses in various sectors in Africa. We also offer consulting services, UAV building and system integration, pilot and safety training, and maintenance of UAVs."*

[The Story] Eric Rutayisire, founder of Charis UAS, was introduced to drone technology by his mentor Kin Chan while studying at the University of Minnesota, Twin Cities. Eric learned how to build drones and brought one home to Rwanda after graduating. He used it to take aerial footage of weddings and concerts before creating Charis UAS, Rwanda's first licensed unmanned aircraft system (UAS) company, with cofounders Teddy Segore and Ingabire Muziga Mamy and a team that holds over forty years of combined experience in aviation. The company builds unmanned aerial vehicles (UAVs) and provides drone solutions across sectors including agriculture, construction, energy, health, tourism and mining. It has used machine learning to identify mosquito breeding sites and undertake targeted drone insecticide spraying to reduce malaria transmission.

Charis UAS now operates in five countries in Africa and is focused on finding new ways to disrupt industries and bring drone services to more people. This means intensive research and even pilot projects done at no cost to the client to prove the efficacy of using a drone solution. Charis UAS also has plans to start manufacturing drones customized to meet the specific needs of the continent.

[Funding History]

Bootstrap   Pre-Seed

Charis UAS was initially self-funded by founder Eric Rutayisire, who used his tax refunds to cover startup costs. The business has since been self-sustaining thanks to its corporate and government contracts and has attracted other undisclosed investments.

[Milestones]
- Scaling to operate in five countries: Côte d'Ivoire, Gabon, Rwanda, Tanzania and Uganda.
- Becoming the first certified UAV company based in Rwanda.
- Launching our first-ever drone made in Rwanda in February 2020.
- Providing aerial imagery of the twenty-fifth Rwandan National Liberation Day commemoration in 2019.

[Links] Web: charisuas.com LinkedIn: company/charis-uas Facebook: charisuas
Instagram: @charissolutionsrw Twitter: @CharisUAS

Charis UAS

startups

[Name] # Exuus

[Elevator Pitch] *"We are a software-development and fintech firm that aims to enable communities to achieve optimal satisfaction by positively impacting the future through technology."*

[The Story] "The drive for me has always been, 'how do I achieve both wealth and impact?'" says Exuus CEO Shema Steve. During a consulting job, he was introduced to savings groups, which are a big part of Rwandan people's financial lives, particularly rural women. Shema was hired to map these informal organizations and visited members, learning about their challenges and gaining an understanding of the role that savings groups could have in much-needed financial inclusion. He developed a platform to address some of these challenges, which would become SAVE.

SAVE enables cashless transactions within savings groups either by USSD or via an app. It allows members to debit or credit the group's digital wallet from their own, individual mobile wallets. NGOs that support savings groups can use the tool to create and manage projects, assign agents to specific areas of intervention and receive real-time information from their agents. With data visible to all, transactions are more transparent, and links to the formal financial sector can be enabled, providing access to additional financial services. For the people using the platform, SAVE means increased agency, societal value and the ability to take more control over their futures and those of their communities.

[Funding History]   Bootstrap   Pre-Seed   Seed

Exuus is a privately held entity and was initially self-funded. It raised pre-seed funding of $95,000 and seed funding of $500,000. Series A funding will allow the startup to scale its offering outside of Rwanda.

[Milestones]
- Launching SAVE, a digital platform to empower savings groups through user-friendly ledger handling.
- Successfully piloting SAVE with over five hundred users in 2018.
- Hitting twenty thousand users and being on the way to one hundred thousand in 2020 and one million in 2021.
- Getting National Bank of Rwanda (BNR) approval to operate.

[Links] Web: exuus.com LinkedIn: company/exuus-ltd Twitter: @exuusLtd

Exuus

[startups]

[Name] # Imagine We

[Elevator Pitch] *"We aim to change reading culture in Rwanda by giving a voice to local authors and allowing them to tell their stories, while also supporting the local literary community with inclusive reading materials."*

[The Story] Dominique Uwase Alonga, CEO of Imagine We, didn't intend to lead a publishing platform. "I think I fell into the work I was doing and it just morphed into other things," she says, referring to her earlier venture, a reading initiative for kids. In this role, she realized that there was a lack of available reading materials for the children she was working with and set up a program for people from around the world to donate books. But many of the titles donated didn't feature characters or plots that felt relevant to Rwandan youth. In response, Dominique established Imagine We, a publishing house that focuses on creating books that reflect Rwandan life. Its titles include stories that address the nation's history of conflict in an age-appropriate way and educational texts that use local references, such as *The ABCs of Rwanda*. Its aim is to change reading culture among children and youth in Rwanda and to give a voice to young authors.

"It's really always evolving," Dominique says, explaining that Imagine We has grown by listening to its consumers and adapting its focus to better meet their needs. The company accelerated its planned shift to digital-first content by launching an app during the country's COVID-19 lockdown. It currently publishes twelve print books a year, but the app enables Imagine We to extend its offerings and gauge the popularity of a story before committing it to print.

[Funding History]

Bootstrap Seed

Imagine We is a self-funded organization. It has received various grants, including $2,000 from Social Impact Incubator Rwanda and $20,000 from the Tigo Digital Changemakers initiative.

[Milestones]
- Winning the $20,000 Tigo Digital Changemakers grant.
- Expanding the team from three to seven people in 2020.
- Launching our app to share many more people's stories.

[Links] Web: imaginewe.rw LinkedIn: company/imagine-we Facebook: ImagineWe
Instagram: imagineiwr Twitter: @ImagineIWR

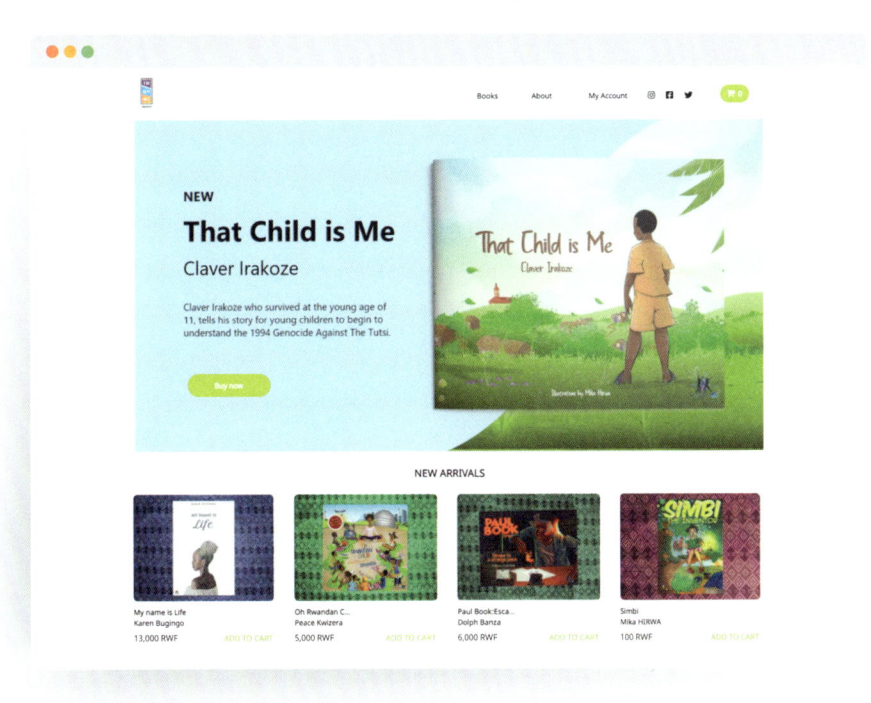

Imagine We

startups

[Name] # Kasha

[Elevator Pitch] *"Kasha is an ecommerce platform for women's health and self-care products. Anyone across the country with a basic mobile phone can browse our products, order and pay, and we deliver confidentially and discreetly to both urban and rural areas."*

[The Story] After working in technology across Africa for a number of years, Joanna Bichsel began to notice a trend. Women, especially those in rural areas, were being left behind. One key element of this was a lack of access to health products such as contraceptives and menstrual care combined with a social stigma about these resources. "Everyone says we should optimize for women, yet women still have a really hard time getting the basic health products they need," Joanna says. "In East Africa there's a very high mobile phone penetration across urban and rural areas and mobile money is more advanced than in other areas of the world. This enables a solution where women can confidentially order products in privacy."

Joanna founded Kasha in 2016. The platform allows women to use their mobile devices to order the products they need and have them delivered directly, cutting out intermediaries and potentially uncomfortable in-person experiences. It now has more than 65,000 customers, and the company has expanded into Kenya while continuing to grow in Rwanda. Kasha aims to be the largest platform in the world for women's health and self-care products and is specifically built for emerging markets.

[Funding History]

Angel · External · Grants · Seed

After receiving initial angel funding from small-scale investors, Kasha has received additional investment from a number of impact-focused VCs, including Sorenson Impact Foundation, East Africa Investments, The Case for Her, VestedWorld and Optimizer Foundation. The company is currently closing a multimillion dollar Series A round led by FinnFund.

[Milestones]
- Surpassing 65,000 customers and selling more than 700,000 product units to customers in urban and rural areas.
- Expanding from Rwanda into Kenya in May 2019.
- Being featured in *Fast Company*'s World Changing Ideas section.

[Links] Web: kasha.co LinkedIn: company/kasha-inc. Facebook: KashaRW
Instagram: KashaRwanda Twitter: @KashaGlobal

Kasha
www.kasha.rw

Kasha
www.kasha.rw

Kasha
Order health products
*911#
www.kasha.rw
9111

Kasha
Kasha

startups

My Green Home

[Name]

[Elevator Pitch] *"We are a social enterprise that uses sand and plastic waste to create durable and environmentally conscious paving bricks. We hope to promote the circular economy and strive for a planet free of plastic waste."*

[The Story] My Green Home was founded in 2017 as the happy by-product of an environmental sustainability class and two bright students who wanted to give back to their communities. Using recycled plastic waste and sand, David Kinzuzi and Rosette Muhoza created an environmentally friendly paving solution that's both durable and affordable. The cofounders competed with over a hundred applicants to receive business coaching from UNICEF Inkomoko Entrepreneur Development, and the company took first place in a UNICEF and Airtel pitch competition. They also won an award at the YouthConnekt Africa Summit in 2018, and the funding received from their success at both of these events allowed them to make My Green Home a viable business.

Since then, David and Rosette have expanded their team and offerings to include services such as delivery and bricklaying. However, it's the process of how each brick is made that's most remarkable. The My Green Home team gathers plastic waste from four collection points across Kigali and sorts it, ensuring that what can't be used goes to another recycling partner. The plastic is washed and shredded, then melted and mixed with sand before being molded. The resulting brick is a highly durable product that represents a step forward in eco-friendly construction.

[Funding History]

Pre-Seed

The founders received $5,000 from the UNICEF Innovation Fund, which financed startup costs. They also received $5,000 as winners of the YouthConnekt Africa Green Growth Innovation Award, which allowed them to increase production capacity.

[Milestones]
- Winning our first grant in 2017, which led to us partnering with notable entities like UNICEF.
- Receiving the Commonwealth Innovation Award, presented by Prince Harry.
- Representing UNICEF Rwanda at a UN conference in Nairobi.
- Participating in the Westerwelle Startup Haus Kigali entrepreneurship program.

[Links] Web: mygreenhome.rw   Twitter: @MyGreenHomeRw   Facebook: MyGreenHomeRwanda

My Green Home

[startups]

[Name] # Rwanda Biosolution

[Elevator Pitch] *"We produce affordable and restorative organic fertilizer by leveraging organic waste and crop residues through effective microorganism technology."*

[The Story] Rwanda Biosolution is a producer of alternatively sourced organic fertilizer. The company uses microorganisms to transform farm and urban organic waste into potent fertilizer that not only improves crop yield but also restores land destroyed by chemical versions. This alternative solution can be produced quickly year-round and is affordable for local farmers. Cofounder Theogene Ingabire says that the team discovered the need for the product at a farming conference in 2015 and then developed its solution at the University of Rwanda's College of Science and Technology. "The results in the lab were so positive that it pushed us to bring out the idea in the real world. That was the birth of Rwanda Biosolution," he says.

Since its foundation, the company has worked with more than a hundred farmers and built a team of six permanent and four part-time employees. Theogene says that it has ambitious plans for the next few years. "My main goal is to serve as many farmers in need of our products as possible, with the key target being to establish a number of agents in five districts. We also want to establish a composting plant in Rwanda that will be able to serve more than two thousand farmers," he says.

[Funding History]   Bootstrap   Grants

Rwanda Biosolution won $1,000 in a business-plan competition organized by DOT Rwanda in 2015. It has since secured $5,000 grant capital from the Tony Elumelu Foundation and $10,000 from the US African Development Foundation, as well as other funding.

[Milestones]
- Partnering with our first farmers, proving that our solution was of value.
- Purchasing a composting machine, which allowed us to increase our production.
- Signing a partnership with One Technical Vocational Training to teach students entrepreneurship in collaboration with educational institutions.
- Launching technical training for farmers on how to best use organic fertilizers, which was important in ensuring uptake.

[Links] Twitter: @RWANDABIOSOLUT1 Facebook: Rwandabiosolution

Rwanda Biosolution

prog

250STARTUPS 52

BPN Rwanda 54

Challenges Rwanda 56

Digital Opportunity
Trust Rwanda 58

G5 Business Makers
Program 60

Hanga Ahazaza 62

Inkomoko Entrepreneur
Development 64

Resonate 66

programs

- Stay innovative and respond to market needs.
  Founders who are able to adapt and apply agile thinking are ideal candidates.

- **Be scalable.**
  Ideally, Rwanda's relatively small market can serve as a test of the product's viability to launch in other countries.

- **Work well with others.**
  Be ready to collaborate or even bring others on board to build a strong team.

- **Ensure that you have a functional business model.**
  A business must be able to make revenue to survive, and founders must be ready to pivot, change or reshuffle should a plan not work.

- **Have a working prototype.**
  Founders are required to have a working prototype when applying to our program.

- **Have an innovative product that involves technology.**
  We're sector-agnostic but require that the solution your business offers be tech-driven.

[Name] # 250STARTUPS

[Elevator Pitch] *"We are an incubation and acceleration program that aims to foster technology startups through mechanisms such as mentorship, market research, business-model development and financial and legal support, among others."*

[Sector] Sector-agnostic

[Description] 250STARTUPS supports early-stage startups that utilize technology. Through a six-month program, the organization helps such companies become investment-ready and supports them as they expand. Each cohort is made up of ten startups with a maximum of two founders and two associates per team, making for a tightly knit group. The program begins with each team conducting market research and validating its product. The teams then develop the products and relevant documentation with the help of associates from legal and financial backgrounds. One-off sessions with guest experts on topics such as design thinking and investment readiness ensure that participants leave with the skills needed to succeed.

At the end of each month in the program, the participating startups present their progress to an audience of investors, partners and other members of the local startup ecosystem, and at the end of the program they get a chance to pitch their solutions to potential investors at a demo day. 250STARTUPS further nurtures the business community by actively recruiting experienced entrepreneurs to be mentors for program participants and by hosting regular events.

Graduates of the program include O'Genius Panda, an education platform with a scientific focus that is scaling up and entering the international scene, and Olado, a web application that provides a route to market for local products through ecommerce.

[Apply to] 250.rw/apply

[Links] Web: 250.rw LinkedIn: company/250STARTUPS Facebook: Startups250
Instagram: 250STARTUPS Twitter: @Startups250

programs

- **Show commitment to the program.**
  Being an entrepreneur is a process, not an end in itself. We want to see evidence of your long-term commitment to the program.

- **Register your company.**
  We are looking for companies that have moved beyond the ideation phase. We want to see that you don't shy away from taking risks.

- **Have a concrete and viable concept.**
  Show us your willingness to work on a sound business plan. Even the most ambitious entrepreneur will struggle without a good concept in place.

- **Prove that it's not just about you.**
  Our program focuses not only on the entrepreneur, but also on how the business can positively impact its community. True to Rwandan culture, we want to see evidence that you will take on social responsibilities.

- **Be scalable.**
  We want to create as many sustainable jobs as possible by working with companies that create value or offer scalable services.

BPN Rwanda

[Elevator Pitch] *"We scout for high-impact entrepreneurs. We embark with them on a flexible, individualized, long-term journey of growth, both personal and business. Our value-based approach focuses on sustainability, profitability and contributing to a sound business culture in developing countries."*

[Sector] Sector-agnostic

[Description] BPN, short for Business Professionals Network, is a non-profit foundation headquartered in Bern, Switzerland. The foundation's goal is to support entrepreneurship in developing countries, and it launched the Rwanda program in October 2011. Alice Nkulikiyinka, BPN Rwanda's country director, advocated for the program to come to Rwanda while working in Switzerland. "I gave up my international career for this beautiful cause," she says.

BPN Rwanda annually selects up to thirty promising SMEs to take part in its entrepreneurship program. These SMEs must have a long-term outlook, a clear vision and have already tested their product or service on the market. The organizations selected often already have a good reputation in their local area. "We identify people with an entrepreneurial mindset. These are people who start something with the purpose of having it grow and making an impact in their community. We aim to be a partner for growth on their entrepreneurial journey," says Alice.

The BPN Rwanda program lasts from two to four years and is based on a four-pillar concept that aims to equip entrepreneurs with the knowledge, security, networking opportunities and financial support to succeed. The four pillars are coaching services, a business academy, a loan scheme and access to an alumni business owner's association. The program is a practical mix of general business support and personalized advice and mentorship. The shoe company Uzuri K&Y is among BPN Rwanda's many success stories. Before entering the program, it was a general fashion company that outsourced production. Mentors at BPN encouraged Uzuri K&Y's two founders to focus the business on one area and bring production in-house. With this new strategy, the company became the largest shoe factory in Rwanda within five years.

[Apply to] bpn.rw

[Links] Web: bpn.rw LinkedIn: company/bpnfoundation Facebook: bpnstiftung

programs

- Be prepared to provide us with data.
  With our in-house internal diagnostics tool, we're able to see whether a company meets our standards while also creating a tailor-made plan for its growth.

- Have solid financial management.
  We aren't just looking for revenue or profit, but for robust financial records and accurate bookkeeping.

- Have a vision for the future.
  We're looking for companies that have a plan. We like to know that the companies we work with have clear goals and ideas on how to meet them.

- Be well organized and well prepared.
  We want companies that are positioned to cope with fluctuations in the market, changes in society and the inherent volatility of people. If you aren't prepared for anything, you won't impress anyone.

[Name] # Challenges Rwanda

[Elevator Pitch] *"We are a development-consultancy firm that offers business-growth services and accredited management training. Working within Rwanda's robust business ecosystem, we've helped both those in the private sector and rural youth."*

[Sector] Sector-agnostic

[Description] Founded in 1999, the Challenges Group is a multinational development consultancy that offers impactful business solutions to SMEs. By collaborating with an established network of NGOs, global banking corporations and government agencies, the organization opens doors and creates opportunities for businesses to build stability and create opportunities for their wider communities. It bridges supply and demand and builds value chains that span entire markets.

Challenges Rwanda was established in 2017 and operates out of Westerwelle Startup Haus Kigali. The organization is dedicated to fostering Rwandan enterprises that have an impactful core concept and it focuses on alleviating youth unemployment. Challenges Rwanda provides guidance and coaching to entrepreneurs, including business diagnostics and market assessment. It works closely with SME business owners to prototype their product or service, identify commercial opportunities and build partnerships. It also offers in-person and online skills development and education, including accredited management training from the Chartered Management Institute.

One of Challenges Rwanda's key initiatives is the Coffee Market Building for Peace and Prosperity project, which offers support to coffee cooperatives in rural areas in southern and western Rwanda to better access the international market. Challenges Rwanda also directly employs talented young professionals in its Kigali office. By doing so, it is able to garner insights into developing markets and attract more young talent, creating a positive ecosystem of attuned professionals. "We seek to build relationships to improve value chains across all of our markets, and value collaboration over competition," says Neil Walker, program manager for Challenges Rwanda. "Not just in our own business-development-service value chain, but across different sectors and verticals such as energy or finance."

[Apply to] rwanda@thechallengesgroup.com

[Links] Web: thechallengesgroup.com LinkedIn: company/challengesrwanda
Facebook: thechallengesgroup Instagram: challengesgroup Twitter: @ChallengesRWA

programs

- **Fit the criteria.**
  Applicants must be recent university graduates aged eighteen to twenty-nine who are unemployed or underemployed.

- **Commit to your community.**
  You need to be committed to work in the location where you are admitted to the program for at least one year.

- **Show passion.**
  Our young people are passionate about community impact and women's development.

- **Be creative.**
  You will be required to come up with innovative digital solutions to community challenges.

- **Adopt a new way of learning.**
  You need to be versatile and willing to learn through a combination of digital and face-to-face lessons.

[Name] # Digital Opportunity Trust Rwanda

[Elevator Pitch] *"We are a youth-led movement empowering social innovators with the tools, knowledge and networks to create opportunities and transform their own communities."*

[Sector] Youth, women

[Description] Digital Opportunity Trust (DOT) was launched in 2001 to support young people in becoming innovators and leaders, and to help them create and apply transformative digital solutions to better their own communities. The organization is youth-led and works in partnership with the private sector, governments and community-based organizations. Globally, its network of six thousand young people has created opportunities for one million people across twenty-five countries.

DOT's Rwandan branch opened in 2010, and its local focus is on job creation and gender equality. DOT Rwanda programs have reached more than eight hundred young people, who have in turn trained more than 100,000 community members. More than 50 percent of its participants are young women. Country director Violette Uwamutara says, "We are incubating young people for them to become leaders and digital and social innovators."

The organization runs a number of programs that advance youth and promote women's empowerment and gender equality. Its flagship offering is the DOT Youth Leadership Program, which encourages young people to develop digital solutions to societal challenges. The program has three aspects. First, it teaches participants competency in digital skills and innovation. Supported by mentors, young people develop the confidence and practical knowledge needed for entrepreneurship. Then, participants use community engagement to better understand local issues and challenges. The third aspect is the social innovation journey, in which DOT provides young people with the social innovation skills needed to develop an MVP for launch to market. The program also helps connect participants with potential investors and mentors. Graduates are encouraged to share their new skills by offering digital and innovation training to their communities, creating a grassroots network of skilled young people.

[Apply to] rwanda@dotrust.org

[Links] Web: rwanda.dotrust.org LinkedIn: company/digital-opportunity-trust
Facebook: DOT Rwanda Twitter: @DOTRwanda Instagram: DOT_Rwanda

programs

- Be ambitious.
  You should be hoping to grow your company or change your career path by taking part in the program.

- Show commitment.
  You should be able to commit the necessary time and pay the program fee.

- Show willingness to learn and grow.
  You should be ready to learn in order to grow either your business venture or your career.

- Be prepared to build long-lasting business relationships.
  Relationships are key for business in our network and this is part of what we help members build.

[Name] # G5 Business Makers Program

[Elevator Pitch] *"We create an innovative ecosystem environment where companies, entrepreneurs, professionals, businesses and students connect to learn, share ideas, solve problems and network."*

[Sector] Sector-agnostic

[Description] The G5 Business Makers Program launched in 2018, when it started hosting its Meet the Professionals events to bring together industry leaders, entrepreneurs, business owners and students to discuss challenges and work on solutions. "At the G5 Business Makers Program, we believe in people and the tremendous contribution they can provide to their workplaces, startups and companies to reshape our companies and society," says founder Christian Kitumaini.

Its scope has expanded since then, but events remain at the heart of the G5 Business Makers Program. To date, it has organized fourteen business summits, which were attended by more than 1,200 guests. The program is not a cohort-based one, but a renewable membership system that features a competitive selection process. To assist companies, it provides access to business mentorship, networking opportunities and market linkage for lead generation opportunities. Professionals looking to launch their own businesses are also welcome to join. G5 works with businesses from any sector and has a focus on helping its members to tackle three of the United Nations Sustainable Development Goals: 8) decent work and economic growth, 9) industry innovation and infrastructure and 17) partnerships for the goals.

Christian says that the G5 Business Makers Program is unique and extremely valuable to both entrepreneurs and aspiring founders, as it puts a premium on mentorship and networking. "We provide mentorship to help you build a sustainable business and to become an innovative changemaker and leader in the industry," he says. "We also help you become part of a network that helps your business build long-lasting relationships."

[Apply to] g5businessmakersprogram.com/membership

[Links] Web: **g5businessmakersprogram.com** LinkedIn: **company/g5-business-makers-program**
Facebook: **G5BMP** Twitter: **@G5BMP** Instagram: **g5bmp**

programs

- **Fit the criteria.**
  We are looking for women- and youth-led businesses that want to speed their development through training.

- **Create jobs.**
  Your business should have the potential to make a meaningful contribution to job creation in Rwanda.

- **Be innovative.**
  We are seeking innovative businesses in terms of use of technology or business model.

- **Show you can scale.**
  The companies we support are those that can demonstrate real potential to scale.

[Name] # Hanga Ahazaza

[Elevator Pitch] *"We are a $50 million initiative from the Mastercard Foundation to increase employment opportunities for thirty thousand Rwandan youth in the tourism and hospitality sector."*

[Sector] Tourism and hospitality

[Description] Hanga Ahazaza means "create the future" in Kinyarwanda and that's exactly what the organization aims to do. Launched in 2018 by the Mastercard Foundation, it is focused on stimulating job creation for young Rwandans by providing skills programs and work opportunities and by supporting small businesses.
The organization identified tourism and hospitality as a focus sector and brought together a consortium of partners from the education, development, financial services and private sectors to achieve its goals.

"Hanga Ahazaza is supporting entrepreneurs with small businesses in the tourism and hospitality sector through increased access to financial services and business development skills training so that they can create new employment opportunities for young people," says Rica Rwigamba, country head for Rwanda at the Mastercard Foundation. "It provides the right skills and accompanies these entrepreneurs to access finance." A $50 million initiative, Hanga Ahazaza backs a variety of programs that provide services to startups at different stages, including AMI, ESPartners and Inkomoko Entrepreneur Development. There are various options for entrepreneurs to receive support specific to the needs of their company and a range of tools and training to help businesses grow. "What makes it unique is the integrated approach that Hanga Ahazaza uses," says Rica. "It also helps businesses find qualified staff who are being trained by other Hanga Ahazaza partners in the education sector. This provides end-to-end support that responds to the youth employment challenge in a holistic manner."

Hanga Ahazaza has supported hundreds of businesses and created thousands of jobs. It encourages job seekers, employees looking to upgrade their skills in tourism and hospitality management, and small business owners to apply for support, particularly those who are young women. Rica says, "Hanga Ahazaza partners are providing support to early-stage entrepreneurs from conception to validation, with a focus on young women. They are also building a platform and a community where aspiring women entrepreneurs are supported and trained to become tomorrow's champions in tourism."

[Apply to] mastercardfdn.org/how-to-apply-to-hanga-ahazaza

[Links] Web: mastercardfdn.org/all/hanga-ahazaza Facebook: MastercardFoundation
Instagram: @mastercardfoundation Twitter: @mastercardfdn

programs

- **Have a functioning product.**
  You need to be past the idea stage, with at least an MVP ready to enter the market.

- **Have specific business requirements.**
  You should be looking for support in a specific area, such as sales and marketing or finance and tax.

- **Be distinctly Rwandan.**
  We are a Rwanda-registered company and your business needs to be registered with the Rwanda Development Board.

- **Show potential for job creation.**
  Your business needs to demonstrate its ability to create employment opportunities.

Inkomoko Entrepreneur Development

[Name]

[Elevator Pitch] "We are a leading SME consulting firm supporting micro, small and medium-sized businesses in Rwanda by offering a four-month accelerator program to equip entrepreneurs with the knowledge and tools to help them grow their businesses."

[Sector] Tourism, hospitality, agribusiness

[Description] Founded in 2012, Inkomoko Entrepreneur Development is an affiliate of African Entrepreneur Collective, a US-based nonprofit organization supporting entrepreneurs across East Africa to stimulate job creation and economic growth. Inkomoko offers entrepreneurs in tourism, hospitality and agribusiness practical solutions to increase their sales and improve their financial management. Its four-month accelerator program begins with an assessment to identify each business' most important needs. Participants then take part in a two-day boot camp to receive training on key concepts and best practices in marketing and finance, before heading into an intense consulting period where they work one-on-one with expert advisors to achieve the objectives set out during the assessment period.

The program is designed to help businesses grow sustainably and to assist entrepreneurs in accessing finance. It does this by preparing participants for external investment and connecting them with potential investors. To date, Inkomoko has worked with almost seven hundred SMEs in Rwanda, creating more than 2,500 jobs. Entrepreneurs who have taken part in the program report valuing the focus on individual needs and the direct impact they see, such as increases in customer base and access to accurate financial reports to better analyze their business. Managing director Nathalie Niyonzima says that, on average, businesses joining Inkomoko increase their revenue by 70 percent and that the program offers a unique combination of intensive business-development support and access to finance. "It is a very practical and individually customized program, where entrepreneurs are coached and trained directly in their businesses to be able to bring about the change needed for growth," she says.

To participate in Inkomoko's program, businesses must be in tourism, hospitality or agribusiness, must have been in operation for at least six months and should show potential for job creation. Entrepreneurs selected to work with Inkomoko also receive access to affordable financing provided by AEC Rwanda Trustee Ltd.

[Apply to] info@inkomoko.com

[Links] Web: inkomoko.com LinkedIn: company/inkomoko-entrepreneur-development
Facebook: inkomoko Instagram: inkomoko Twitter: @inkomoko

programs

- **Engage with our business-to-business model.**
  We work with NGOs, companies and other groups that would like their members to acquire hard skills and combine them with empowering soft skills.

- **Provide training in hard skills for the workplace and beyond.**
  We bring soft skills training to partner organizations that upskill women in hard skills.

- **Work with vulnerable youth.**
  We aim to partner with organizations that work with women and youth in rural areas, particularly those who have previously had a lack of access to formal training.

- **Have a desire for growth.**
  We provide training that amplifies the value that employees and team members bring to a growing organization.

[Name] # Resonate

[Elevator Pitch] *"Resonate provides leadership workshops that allow women to build their confidence, shift their mindsets, turn skills into action and fulfill their potential. By coupling hard skills with leadership training, we amplify our partners' impact and the benefits to the women and girls we serve."*

[Sector] Education

[Description] Founded in 2013, Resonate aims to address the confidence gap: the opportunities that women and girls miss out on when they underestimate their abilities. It partners with organizations that provide hard-skills training to women and girls – often those in marginalized, rural communities – and ensures that participants are equipped with soft skills to help them get to a position to use their training. With storytelling methods adapted for a Rwandan context and using a Harvard-developed model, Resonate lets each learner find her individual strengths and harness them to achieve her goals. The organization teaches that leadership is about proactively finding solutions to problems and creating a positive impact, not simply about holding a formal leadership position.

Resonate teaches three programs with specific objectives: Storytelling for Leadership teaches women to speak up and share ideas in a group environment, and has a focus on decision-making skills; Action Leadership works with young people to provide experience in designing and implementing community projects; and the Professional Development program teaches soft skills for high-potential employees, developing talent in the workplace by enabling effective planning and prioritization. In 2019, Resonate reported that 37 percent of its graduates had started businesses, 73 percent had taken on a leadership role and 30 percent had received a new academic opportunity, job or promotion.

The team behind Resonate aims to increase the reach and impact of its programs. The company has a scalable growth plan that trains facilitators and contracts those who are identified as having exceptional training skills. Currently, it operates with the support of US donors, but is on its way to being self-sufficient, with around 20 percent of its revenue currently coming from companies employing its services.

[Apply to] admin@resonateworkshops.org

[Links] Web: resonateworkshops.org LinkedIn: company/resonateworkshops
Facebook: resonateworkshops Instagram: rworkshops Twitter: @Rworkshops

spa

ces

FabLab Rwanda 70

Impact Hub Kigali 74

kLab 76

WAKA 78

Westerwelle Startup Haus Kigali 82

spaces

[Name] # FabLab Rwanda

[Address] Telecom House, 6th Floor, 8 KG 7 Ave., Kacyiru, Kigali

[Total Area]

278 M²

[Workspaces]

50

Depending on projects

[The Story] FabLab aims to provide innovative individuals with access to cutting-edge digital fabrication laboratories almost anywhere in the world. These labs are more than just places to build a product – the organization also encourages members to mentor one another, share ideas and collaboratively realize impactful concepts. Through providing such spaces, the initiative is fostering a generation of bright minds who want to build a better future.

FabLab Rwanda was founded in 2016 as a collaboration between the Rwanda Development Board, Japan International Cooperation Agency, Rwanda's Ministry of Education, SolidWorks Corporation MIT-CBA and Gasabo 3D to support the creation of hardware and electronics by local innovators. Participants typically use a four-step process to create a product: ideation; design and simulations to see what changes might need to be made; prototyping the product; and lab and customer testing as well as any refinement. FabLab Rwanda helps its members with every step of the process and provides funding. It also assists in the creation of business models and connects creators with investors. FabLab Rwanda members have built everything from drones to educational materials. In 2018, the organization pivoted to a more business-oriented approach, seeking to help develop startups with marketable ideas and spread their impact across the continent.

[Links] Web: fablab.rw Facebook: KigaliFabLab Instagram: fablab_rwanda Twitter: @fablabRW

FabLab Rwanda

spaces

FabLab Rwanda

Face of the Space:
Lambert Rulindana joined FabLab Rwanda in August 2016, just three months after its foundation. He's participated in numerous courses and the production of everything from drones to spacecraft. With a bachelor's degree in electronics and telecommunication engineering, he's also been able to teach countless others and is now the space's general manager.

spaces

[Name] # Impact Hub Kigali

[Address] The Office, 3rd and 4th Floors, 34 KN 41 St., Kiyovu, Kigali

[Total Area]

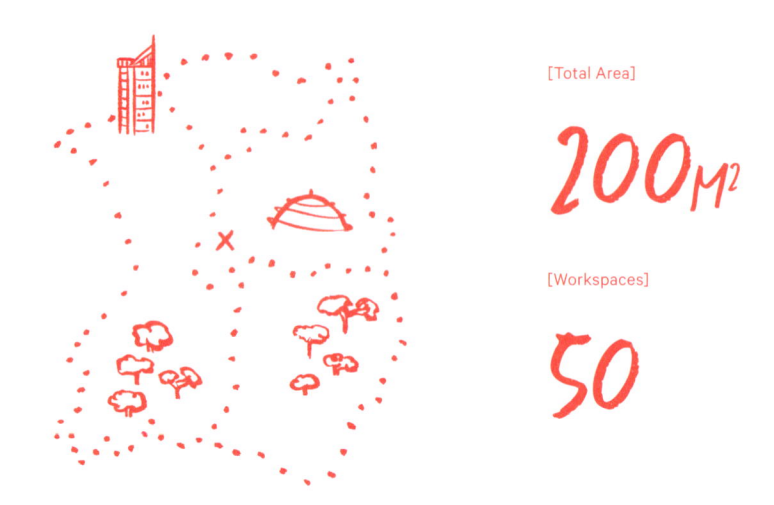

200 M²

[Workspaces]

50

[The Story] Headquartered in Vienna, the Impact Hub network of coworking spaces was designed to support startups with solutions that contribute to social and economic development. The Kigali location launched in August 2015. It offers workspace with high-speed internet, a spacious meeting room and a roof terrace that can accommodate up to 150 people. "The moment you walk into Impact Hub Kigali, you realize how unique a space it is. Our love for arts and culture immediately stands out, as our building is covered with colorful murals and paintings by artists from Rwanda and the region," says Cares Manzi, the space's manager.

As with all Impact Hubs, the organization is about more than coworking. Members have access to weekly events, where they can connect with a wider community of innovators and changemakers. They can also take part in innovation-catalyzing programs, which can help participants develop ideas and create pitches for funding and mentorship. "From the very beginning, we believed in collaboration as a main driver of innovation and positive change. We are unique in that we bring together people with diverse backgrounds, from creatives to tech experts, from dancers to environment enthusiasts, from entrepreneurs to public officials, from innovators to diplomats, and everyone in between," Cares says.

[Links] Web: kigali.impacthub.net LinkedIn: company/impact-hub-kigali
Facebook: impacthubkigali Instagram: impacthubkigali Twitter: @ImpactHubKigali

Impact Hub Kigali

Face of the Space:
Cares Manzi has managed Impact Hub Kigali and organized community events since 2017. He is passionate about connecting people and has expertise in developing innovation-catalyzing programs for the Rwandan entrepreneurial ecosystem.

spaces

[Name] kLab

[Address] Telecom House, 6th Floor, 8 KG 7 Ave., Kacyiru, Kigali

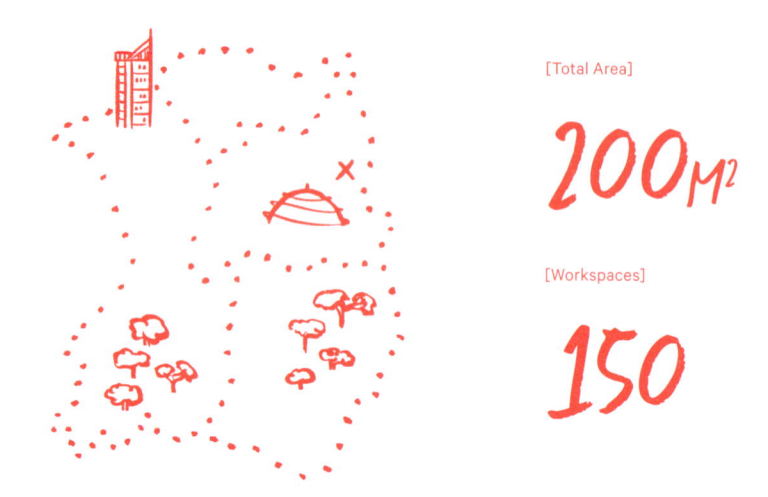

[Total Area]

200 M²

[Workspaces]

150

[The Story] When kLab opened in 2012, the government-funded enterprise was the first innovation space in Kigali. Located at the top of Telecom House and with a 360-degree view of the city, the organization helps young entrepreneurs and students to turn their ideas into viable businesses. Its two thousand members can access the space 24/7, and it's free to use.

kLab is central to the Rwandan government's goal of establishing a knowledge-based economy and fostering innovative ICT-based SMEs. "kLab is at the bottom of the pyramid," says Aphrodice Mutangana, the space's general manager. In addition to providing internet access and workspace for 150 people at a time, kLab offers access to a 500-strong mentorship community that provides both technical and business assistance to members. The hub also hosts a variety of events, workshops, boot camps, hackathons and networking sessions to encourage collaboration, partnerships and investments. "kLab's mission is to promote, facilitate and support the development of innovative ICT solutions by nurturing a vivid community of entrepreneurs and mentors," Aphrodice says.

[Links] Web: klab.rw LinkedIn: company/klab-rw Facebook: klabrw
Instagram: klabrwanda Twitter: @klabrw

kLab

Face of the Space:

Aphrodice Mutangana is kLab's general manager and a co-initiator of Future Coders, Incike Initiative and the Refugee School of Coding. He sits on the boards of numerous organizations related to innovation and entrepreneurship.

spaces

[Name] WAKA

[Address] KN 72 St., Kigali

[Total Area]

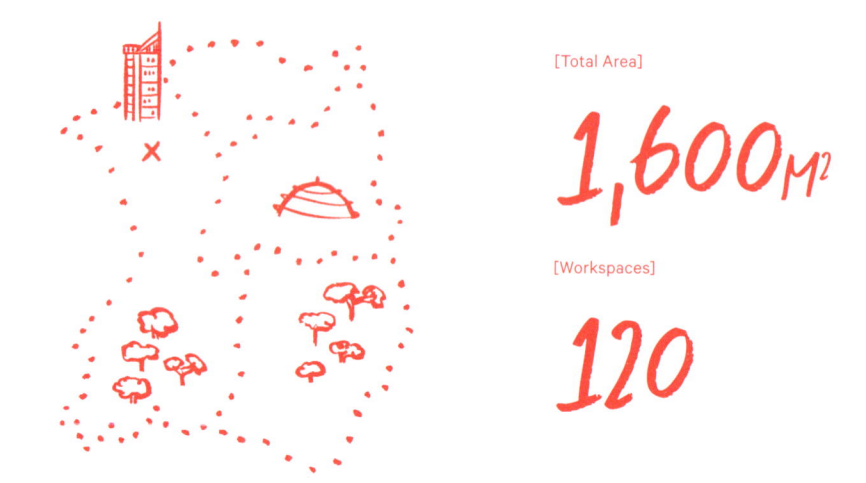

1,600 M²

[Workspaces]

120

[The Story] Whether they're hard-core fitness enthusiasts or entrepreneurs looking for a fresh approach to work–life balance, WAKA members enjoy a host of facilities that support a holistic lifestyle. The multifunctional space was founded in 2014 by Jeannetta Craigwell-Graham and Dennis Dybdal, a Danish-American expat couple who couldn't find a gym in Kigali to suit their needs. WAKA is a modern coworking space with private offices, hot desks and high-speed internet, but it's also home to a well-equipped gym, basketball court and bouldering wall. An in-house cafe serves meals designed by a registered dietician, and a physiotherapist is available. Classes and member events are designed to be inclusive, with options such as prenatal and postpartum workouts and regular family fun days.

Since its launch, the WAKA community has grown from 250 members to nearly 2,000. There's a waiting list to sign up as the organization continues in its mission to push the boundaries of professional spaces. The WAKA team prides itself on remaining flexible and attuned to the needs of members, which has allowed the space to grow and adapt alongside the companies and individuals who work there.

[Links] Web: wakaglobal.com Facebook: wakarwanda Instagram: WAKAglobal Twitter: @WAKA_Global

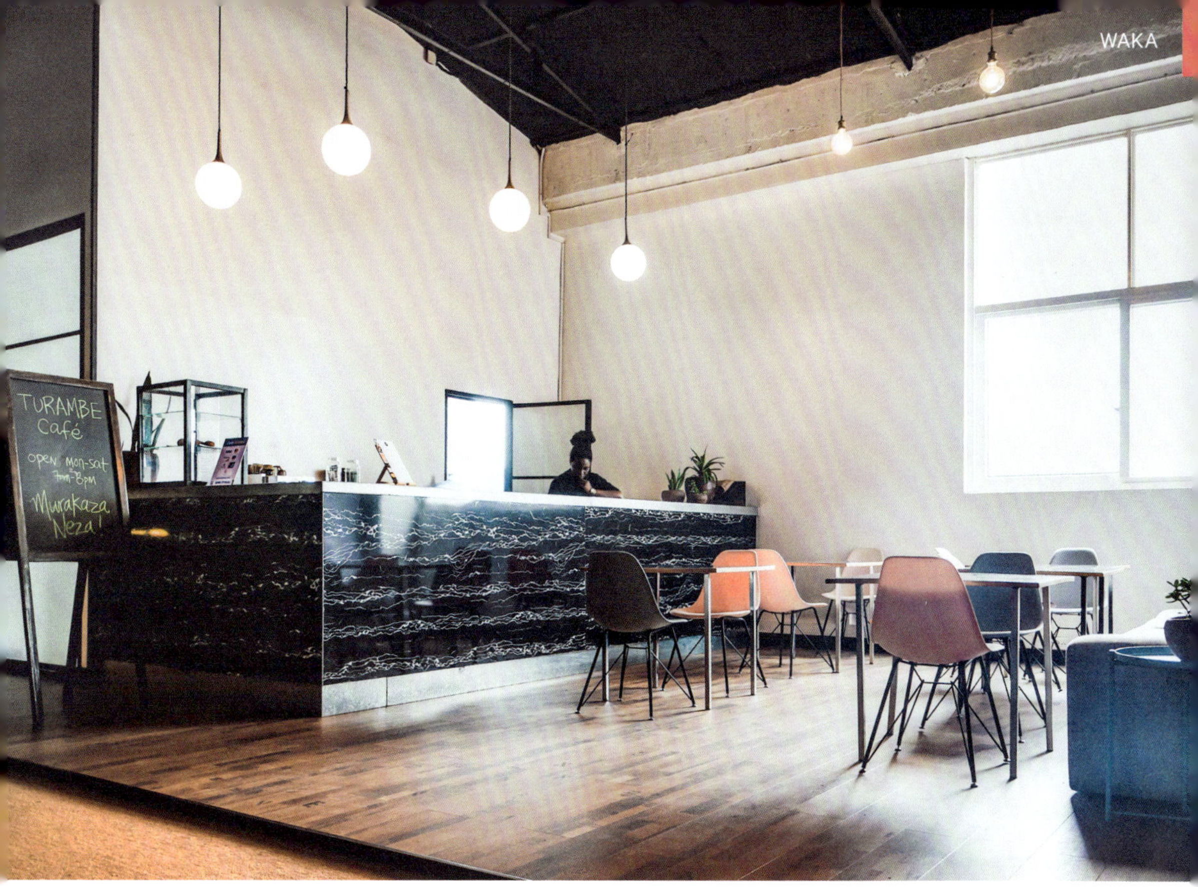
TURAMBE
Café
open Mon-Sat
7am-8pm
Murakaza
Neza!

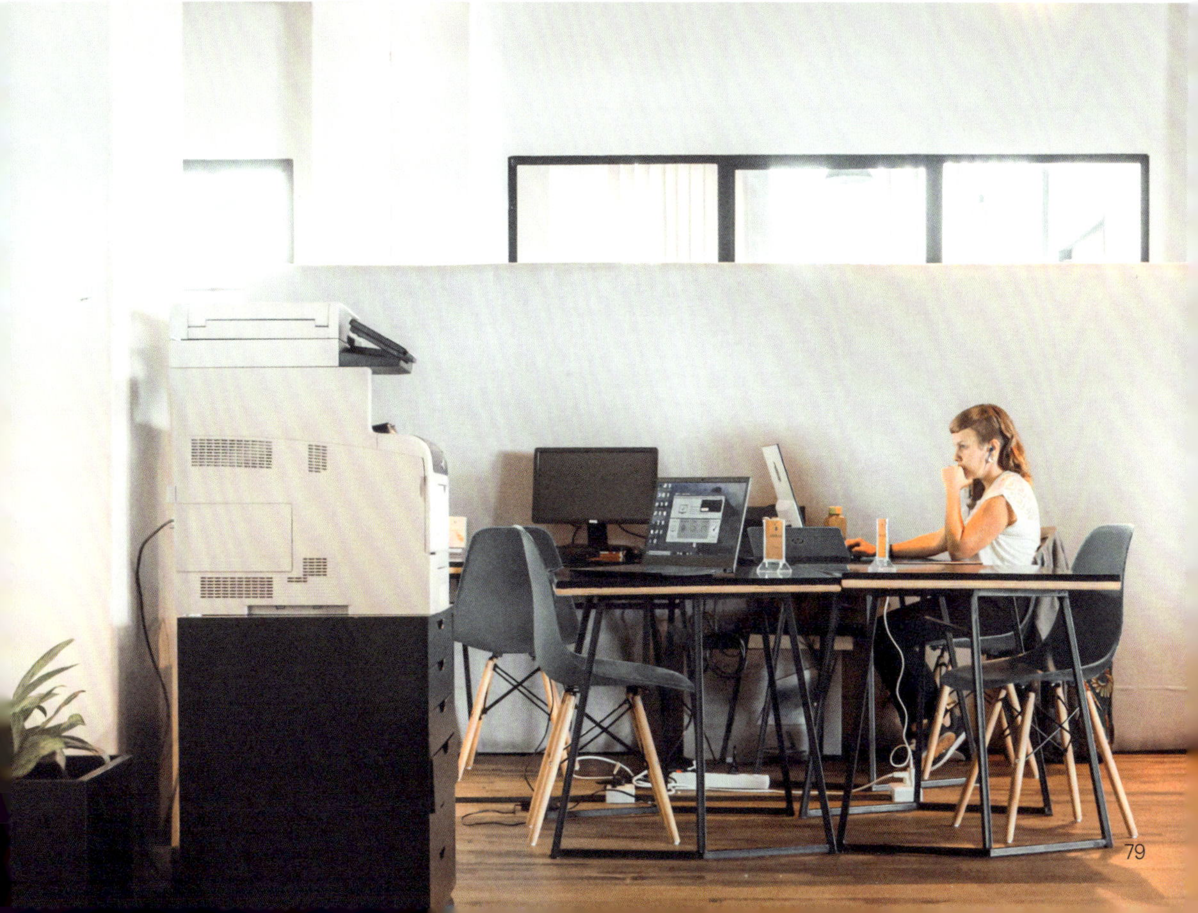

spaces

Face of the Space:

Community manager Nathalie Bintu has worked with WAKA since 2019. Holding a bachelor's degree in water and environmental engineering from the University of Rwanda, she worked as a water production and quality technician before making her move to the customer service industry a few years ago.

spaces

[Name] # Westerwelle Startup Haus Kigali

[Address] Fairview Building, 4th and 5th Floor, KG 622 St., Kigali

[Total Area]

1,200 M²

[Workspaces]

170

[The Story] Launched in 2018, Westerwelle Startup Haus Kigali is an innovative coworking space offering desks and private offices alongside a host of amenities conducive to productivity and business growth. High-speed internet, printing services, conference rooms and private phone booths are available to members. It also has a terrace with an impressive view of the city. The space is powered by the Evonik Foundation and operated by the Westerwelle Foundation with an aim of fostering economic growth in the region by supporting young entrepreneurs and creating new economic opportunities.

An on-site makerspace is equipped with tools including a laser cutter and 3D printers, making it easy for members to create prototypes and collaborate with others who are specialized in production. There is also ample opportunity to make connections at community events. The space is a venue for team-building sessions, weekly informal discussions of challenges and highlights, networking drinks, breakfasts and other meetups. Westerwelle Startup Haus Kigali also offers a six-month entrepreneurship program that supports selected startups with training in finances and planning, as well as business diagnostic sessions and access to legal and financial support services.

[Links] **Web:** kigali.westerwelle.haus **LinkedIn:** company/westerwelle-startup-haus-kigali
Facebook: wshkigali **Instagram:** wsh_kigali **Twitter:** @WSH_Kigali

Westerwelle Startup Haus Kigali

spaces

Westerwelle Startup Haus Kigali

Face of the Space:

Operations manager Blaise Dusi leads the entrepreneurship program and is passionate about community empowerment. He works with Rwanda Toastmasters Club to help members improve their communication and leadership skills.

Sarah Rukundo is a senior manager who is focused on building an active community of entrepreneurs and mentors. She organizes events and workshops. Sarah holds an MBA in project management from Oklahoma Christian University and loves to travel.

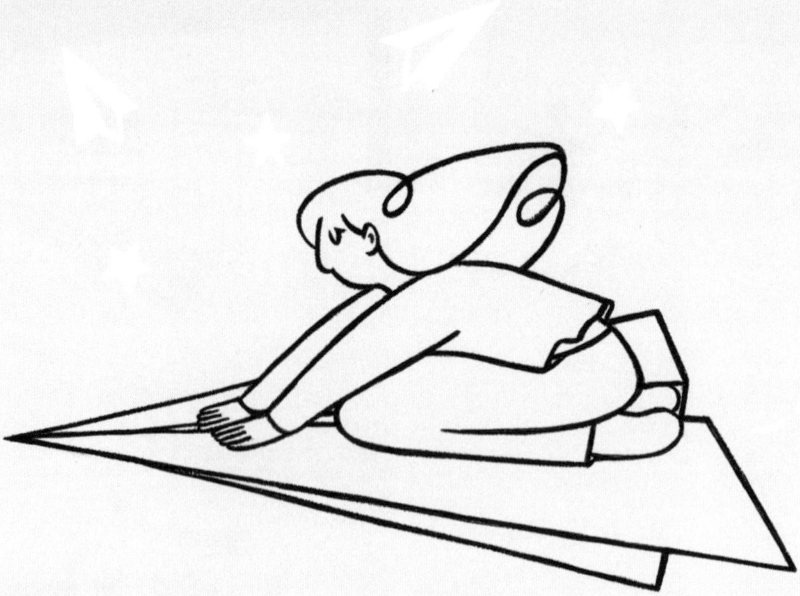

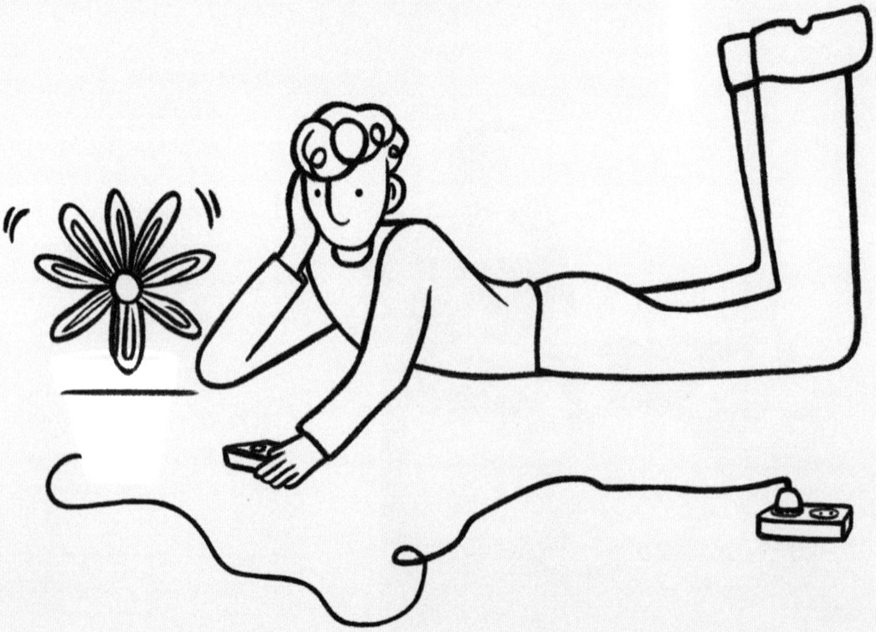

SAP

Segal Family Foundation

experts

In partnership with **SAP**

Leveraging Technology to Overcome Adversity

Hardeep Sound / Regional Leader, East Africa, SAP

[Sector]   Enterprise application software

During a large-scale medical emergency or other crisis, a country's government, private sector and communities are put under pressure and vulnerabilities are exposed. These groups must work to fill immediate gaps as quickly as possible, creating solutions and initiatives in a short amount of time, but they can struggle to work together.

"You have communities, societies and government entities that have disconnected initiatives, rarely collaborate well or share information and don't have a collective objective," says Hardeep Sound, regional leader for East Africa at SAP. Hardeep started his career at Deloitte and worked for Microsoft and Oracle in various consulting and sales positions in his decades-long career. He joined SAP in October 2019 to explore leadership challenges in addition to sales. In 2020, he witnessed countries in the region he covers react to the COVID-19 outbreak and saw how technology can be a great enabler and bring solutions to citizens. He reports seeing local innovators harness technology to solve immediate problems and bridge gaps.

Hardeep points to Health-E-Net, a Kenyan startup that provides patients with a telemedicine platform to access a global network of volunteer medical professionals, and MyDawa, a Nairobi-based app that allows individuals to purchase medical supplies. MomCare is another example. The SMS solution was created by the PharmAccess Foundation, which has offices in Kenya, Nigeria, Ghana and Tanzania. It provides medical services and resources, such as emergency transport to hospitals, to pregnant women in an effort to reduce maternal mortality.

COVID-19 disrupted supply chains and operations around the world, but Hardeep highlights how technology can reduce the impact of such large-scale disturbance and provide solutions. "SAP has Ariba Network, which minimizes disruptions in production supply chains," he says. "It allows any buyer to post immediate sourcing needs and any of the four million suppliers can respond to communicate their ability to deliver needed goods and services."

experts

In partnership with **SAP**

Most important tips for startups:

- **Leverage existing technology.** Creating your own software solution takes a lot of time, effort and funding. Use proven technology as a tool, such as software as a service or infrastructure as a service solutions, to have a more immediate impact.

- **Work on an OPEX model.** Optimize for your day to day operating expenses by using pay-as-you-go software as much as possible to manage your cash flow. This works better than a CAPEX model when starting up.

- **Invest in your employees.** Enable them to achieve their fullest capacity using continuous development, and consider opening up equity for employees right from the beginning.

- **Align your business with the UN's sustainable development goals.** Depending on your business, it can be important to present and have a social element.

experts

Hardeep notes that it's important for companies to seek feedback from customers and use this first-hand information from the people on the ground to continually adapt and improve. "That enables a lot of trust between citizens and medical providers or governments who are providing these services," he says. Technology can enable the quick collection of feedback and help organizations make more informed decisions.

Hardeep recommends that startups create an end-to-end process to understand what citizens really need. This involves gathering insights on the market, building an action plan and understanding the impact once the product or service is live. Then, he suggests creating case studies and references to sustain the momentum. To achieve this, Hardeep advises startups to use technology that's already on the market rather than creating a solution from scratch. Using proven technology can be more efficient and bring faster results. There are a number of technology providers, including SAP, that have software solutions to help startups grow on a pay-as-you-go model, and that only require configuration to get started.

Founders should think about how they can leverage technology as a strategic enabler to help them achieve their required impact, Hardeep says. "Businesses must not invest in technology for technology's sake, because it's a trend. Use it because it's going to provide the impact you need for your business to grow and become scalable." He suggests that companies develop a customer-centric culture where product and service improvement are the priorities, and that they use technology as a tool to achieve this.

About

SAP has evolved to become a market leader in end-to-end enterprise application software, database, analytics, intelligent technologies and experience management. A top cloud company with 200 million users worldwide, SAP helps businesses of all sizes and in all industries to operate profitably, adapt continuously and achieve their purpose.

[Contact] Email: hardeep.sound@sap.com Telephone: +254 700 070 080

[Links] Web: sap.com/africa LinkedIn: company/sap Facebook: SAP Instagram: sap Twitter: @SAPAfrica

In partnership with **SAP**

"*Businesses must not invest in technology for technology's sake. Use it because it's going to provide the impact you need for your business to grow and become scalable.*"

experts

In partnership with **Segal Family Foundation**

Creating a Thriving Entrepreneurial Ecosystem

Liana Nzabampema / Senior Program Officer, Segal Family Foundation

[Sector]   Philanthropy

In recent years, Rwanda has invested substantially in creating policies that foster a thriving entrepreneurial ecosystem. "Rwanda sets the example globally in its approach to creating value and opportunities beyond the public and private sector," says Liana Nzabampema, senior program officer at Segal Family Foundation. "We continue to see efforts aimed at creating a space for entrepreneurship and entrepreneurs to thrive. There are so many examples, but let's focus on the process of registering a business, which is now really at the fingertips of entrepreneurs. This is certainly manifested in the visible growing market and zero tolerance corruption policies taken seriously by the government."

Liana joined Segal Family Foundation in 2016, having spent many years working in international development across Africa and Australia. In Rwanda, she leads the foundation's Social Impact Incubator and approaches value creation for entrepreneurs through an ecosystem lens. Segal Family Foundation is on a mission to unlock massive potential for African social entrepreneurs and Rwanda offers an ideal setup to experiment before scaling the concept to other countries.

Rwanda has a young population with a lot of entrepreneurial potential. To harness this demographic's creativity and aspirations, Liana says that tailored regulations, platforms, financial instruments and programs must be thoughtfully created. Segal Family Foundation has been committed to investing in this space through its Social Impact Incubator since 2019.

The incubator's focus is on investing in entrepreneurs and the socio-economic environment they live in. According to Liana, this is the only way to build businesses and entrepreneurs that will in five to ten years' time sustainably serve and support their communities. "The youth are putting their focus and energy into non-traditional ways of doing business – creating wealth but also addressing social issues that had previously affected the process of doing business," she says. "These are hybrid ways of responding to the challenges around them, with agile and flexible business models that provide them with control and a sense of sustainability."

experts

In partnership with Segal Family Foundation

Most important tips for startups:

- **Don't start a business because you can't get a job.** Some of the best businesses have been built out of frustration, but what makes them sustainable is the entrepreneurial drive of the founders.

- **Learn from your failures.** It's okay to fail when building your startup, just keep failing forward, learning and growing.

- **Do your research.** Don't rely on stories. Do the research to understand the problem you're solving, who it's for and where it fits in the future.

- **Be patient.** It takes time for any business to gain momentum, and it's the perseverance to innovate, hard work and hope that will keep you going.

- **Cultivate a community:** Find peers you can lean on and who always push you to the next level on your entrepreneurial journey.

experts

The Social Impact Incubator is an intensive seven-month program, during which participants take part in Think Pods, workshops covering everything from service and product development, financial models, design, communication, fundraising, impact measurement and business development. "It's a platform that nurtures leadership and innovation," says Liana. "We build human capital and create bonds amongst entrepreneurs as well as to the right sector experts through coaching and mentorship. In the background, we continue developing in-roads to funders, investors and policy makers."

"Our goal is to create an environment where entrepreneurs, regardless of their registration, can find skills, build networks and access agile and blended capital that propels them to succeed," she continues. "We are also historically known for our ultimate networking experiences. We see these diverse efforts paying off and are slowly bringing together a community, network and burgeoning ecosystem of entrepreneurs, working closely with the public and private sector, fulfilling the government priorities and SDGs."

Powered by Segal Family Foundation and Robert Bosch Stiftung, the Social Impact Incubator's ultimate goal is to advocate for increased funding options for early-stage entrepreneurs across Africa. "While the capacity gap has always been used as a proxy to not fund or take risks, it's going to be hard addressing the slow growth of African entrepreneurs unless we see it as a predicament funders and investors need to solve, particularly looking at how they structure their financing schemes," Liana says. She also notes that ecosystem-builders need to do more to support entrepreneurs. "Continuing to offer the same programs and small grants over and over without underpinning the causes of the volatility in the sector might be disingenuous," she says. "This is the only guarantee to not have the same story over and over. Am I asking for fresh perspectives and new narratives? Absolutely!" She suggests creating a value chain for entrepreneurs where they are supported through each step of their business, from ideation to expansion, in the ways that are most appropriate and sustainable for their particular circumstances.

About

Segal Family Foundation is a private philanthropic foundation that partners with African organizations and visionaries to transform communities. Since 2008, it has provided strategic support and grants to over two hundred partner organizations across sub-Saharan Africa. Its unique collaborative approach to philanthropy gives communities the power to make their own decisions and leads to lasting change.

[Contact] Email: liana@segalfamilyfoundation.org Telephone: +250 781 469 890

[Links] Web: segalfamilyfoundation.org LinkedIn: company/segal-family-foundation
Facebook: SegalFamilyFoundation Twitter: @SegalFoundation

In partnership with **Segal Family Foundation**

> *Our goal is to create an environment where entrepreneurs regardless of their registration, can find skills, build networks and access agile and blended capital that propels them to succeed.*

foun

Christelle Kwizera / Water Access Rwanda **102**

Clarisse Iribagiza / DMM.HeHe **110**

Henri Nyakarundi / ARED **118**

Patrick Buchana Nsenga / AC Group **126**

founders

Christelle Kwizera

Managing Director / Water Access Rwanda

In Rwanda, two out of three people live in poverty and access to safe water is a challenge. Christelle Kwizera, the founder of Water Access Rwanda, made it her mission to change this through social entrepreneurship and technology. While in her third year of university, she embarked on a summer project to tackle the clean water crisis, and after seeing her solutions make a difference, she formally launched Water Access Rwanda in 2014. Since then, Christelle has provided water solutions to communities throughout Rwanda and in other East African countries, and has changed the landscape of social entrepreneurship in Kigali and beyond.

How did you become interested in engineering as well as impact and social entrepreneurship?
I have always been interested in entrepreneurship. Something about taking risks and growing the value of ideas and companies always appealed to me. Even when I was young and couldn't quite process what it was all about, I was always making money at every opportunity I found. I put on dance performances for visitors at home, I sold celebrity posters to classmates and I charged my dad when I helped him out with his work. My path to engineering was a little more complicated. I received great grades in school and that actually kind of limited me to three fields, in the African parenting sense of things: medicine, law and engineering. I have always been in love with aerospace engineering and I had eyed several great aerospace engineering schools, such as Embry-Riddle. I even got accepted there, but unfortunately didn't get enough scholarships to be able to afford it. Fascinated by watching MacGyver make bombs out of everyday objects in order to escape tricky situations, I decided instead to pursue mechanical engineering. I got accepted to attend Oklahoma Christian University and received enough scholarships to fund my education.

How did you come to find your clean water focus?
The connection to water and geophysics came during my third year of university. During what should have been a summer project to drill for clean water, I found a life calling: to end the water crisis and youth unemployment. However, up until the time we arrived in the community and started drilling, it all felt a bit impersonal to me. I was doing the finance, the planning, training people and working on the tech side, but at that point the number of people who didn't have access to clean water was just a number for me. I hadn't really seen their faces.

Christelle Kwizera / Water Access Rwanda

When I was very young, my family struggled with access to clean water, but I only associated it with outages once in a while. It was eye-opening for me to go into this community and see people who had never had access to clean piped water. The only water source within a ten kilometer radius provided unclean water, and that unclean water contained crocodiles. The local school there had a low pass rate for national exams, and I wondered whether this was connected to the water supply. Research found that the water contained huge amounts of lead, and if you consume lead from a very young age, you will have developmental issues. I learned that thirty percent of children there were stunted, and that this was connected to the lack of access to clean water. I became a better advocate. I understood the problem more and it all started to become more of a reality for me. I decided that I was going to invest my life in this.

What were some of your early challenges while starting up and how did you overcome them?

In the early stages, I had two main challenges. The first was that I was young and everyone treated me like I was a child. The second was that I had to be honest in realizing that my solution was not sustainable. It took a lot of courage to say that UNICEF, the Rotary Foundation and everyone else promoting a model of hand pumps for rural communities was wrong. These are big organizations and it was a challenge to have to admit that I was doing something wrong. I ended up giving myself the credit I needed, and now we have the first borehole-fed rural water mini-grid in the world.

There was also the issue of education in the communities where we installed boreholes. Early on, I was driving by a field and I passed a borehole that worked perfectly, but people were passing it and going to the river. I stopped and asked everybody fetching water in the river why they weren't using the borehole. They said the borehole had worms in it. The river water did too, but it wasn't clear water so they couldn't see them. I later saw a lady drinking water from a river where a man was cleaning himself uphill. I asked why she was drinking that water, and she said it was fine because he was her husband. It was baffling to me that we were providing a solution and still there were so many examples of it not working. I realized there was a need for a bigger presence in the community. You can't just drill and leave. You have to stay. We needed longer-term education and training for using boreholes and pumps.

What do you believe was your biggest mistake, as well as your best decision as a founder?

The biggest mistake I made was to enter into a long-term professional partnership without putting down the terms in writing first. The best decision I made was diving into the world of entrepreneurship, a world I did not understand.

> *You have to be humble enough to accept simple beginnings and slow growth. At the same time, you should also be ambitious enough to envision major gains and massive growth.*

founders

How did you make your business model profitable, and can you highlight any early successes in that journey?
Drafting projections before engaging is a key aspect of what I do. The learning points were to see that often the reality is interrupted by many aspects not considered in a model. This has meant that we've had to stay lean and figure out innovative ways to make money that were not in the model we started with. We actually threw out all the models that didn't work, because traditional hand pump business models were not working. We needed to innovate and do better.

Do you have any specific business case examples?
One example of this is when we realized that boreholes cost around two thousand to four thousand dollars, and communities didn't have that money. In 2015, we introduced services such as filters, which were cheaper, so people didn't have to invest in boreholes. We noticed that farmers were more willing and able to afford pipes and water systems. In 2016, because drilling is the core business of the company and the highest revenue source we have, and because we have a passion for giving people safe drinking water and creating employment for young people, we started building waterways for farmers. That way, the community had access to lay pipes, and could pay farmers a small amount so they could buy diesel for their pumps. We established this for a few farmers, and it became a win-win. Because the community had water nearby they didn't have to invest in any infrastructure, and the farmer would receive revenue.

What professional advice would you give to people in the early stages of starting up?
You have to be humble enough to accept simple beginnings and slow growth. At the same time, you should also be ambitious enough to envision major gains and massive growth.

How would you describe the startup ecosystem and community in Kigali?
The ecosystem here is quite nascent. We still have many gaps to fill and not enough exciting startups. Many startups have set their bars quite low, and I feel they could be setting them much higher. In terms of where the ecosystem is headed in the future, we do need more A-players, people who are committed to creating value for businesses in Kigali. I do think it's still growing. Water Access Rwanda has been one of the leading voices of social entrepreneurship here. Before, the focus was on tech entrepreneurs and ICT, and we came in as the first self-described social enterprise in the country. We were able to demonstrate how to combine being for-profit and caring about a cause.

founders

How have you impacted the ecosystem?
I think we established a pretty good standard of what a social enterprise can do in the Rwanda ecosystem. We're really leading in terms of quantifiable impact around different issues, and we're seeing more social entrepreneurs joining the ecosystem. Many young entrepreneurs now prefer to describe themselves as social entrepreneurs. Of course I can't take all the credit – when we started, many other enterprises were being founded at the same time. Now we employ a bunch of the people involved in those original enterprises. We were part of the first generation of young entrepreneurs and had a massive impact in terms of job creation. We're also changing the narrative around making money – it isn't only reserved for mature entrepreneurs. For the ecosystem to grow, you need more players going for big revenue and impact. The ecosystem still has a long way to go.

What are the pillars on which you hire the right people for your team?
Potential team members for Water Access Rwanda have to love what we do above all else. They have to be willing to fail, accept the failure and learn from it. Finally, they should be stubborn in their commitment to our vision.

How do you foster a great team dynamic and culture?
We make sure there is lots of open communication during the work day, and also have parties with great food when we can afford it!

How do you keep yourself inspired and disciplined as a founder?
What keeps me inspired is knowing the impact we can have if we continue to push and also give value to everyone else who has sacrificed something to be with me and the company on this journey.

[About] Created in 2014, Water Access Rwanda is a social enterprise working to put an end to water scarcity via simple technology. The company has provided access to clean water to over 159,000 individuals, schools, farms and businesses in Rwanda, Democratic Republic of the Congo, Uganda and Burundi. To provide lasting solutions for communities, the company offers many services and products, all within the available budget of each region.

[Links] Web: warwanda.com LinkedIn: company/water-access-rwanda
Facebook: waterRwanda Instagram: water_access_rwanda Twitter: @WaterRwanda

Christelle Kwizera / Water Access Rwanda

What are your top work essentials?
A great team that understands ideas and delivers implementation tactics.

At what age did you found your company?
Twenty.

What's your most-used app?
Twitter.

What's the most valuable piece of advice you've been given?
It hurts to have questions and no answers, but equally so to have answers and have nobody to ask.

What's your greatest skill?
Empathy, understanding systems and the courage to challenge the status quo.

founders

Clarisse Iribagiza

CEO and Cofounder / DMM.HeHe

Clarisse Iribagiza was twenty-two years old and still a student when she cofounded DMM.HeHe in 2010. Formerly HeHe Labs before joining DMM.com Group Japan in 2017, DMM.HeHe (colloquially called HeHe) is an innovative tech firm that creates business-optimization solutions, enabling companies across Africa to offer products and services seamlessly on demand. Clarisse cofounded the company with fellow University of Rwanda classmates Richard Rusa, Sixbert Uwiringiyiana and Davy Nshhuti while completing an incubation program organized by Massachusetts Institute of Technology's (MIT) Global Startup Labs. The inspiration to become a tech founder came from her work as a student of computer engineering coupled with her learnings from the MIT incubator, which she felt she could apply to the real world. In addition to her role as CEO, Clarisse is a member of the Presidential Youth Advisory Group at the African Development Bank.

How did you become interested in computer science and impact entrepreneurship? What inspired you to become the founder you are today?
I think my parents had the greatest impact on me. My mother was entrepreneurial and my dad stressed the need to get a good education. They both encouraged me to pursue the things I was passionate about, good at and that could create an impact in the world. As well, from an early age, I had an affinity for technology and loved problem solving. It was when I was working on my computer engineering degree at the University of Rwanda's College of Science and Technology that the nexus of these two passions gave birth to HeHe, which was launched out of an MIT-run incubation program that I was privileged to be a part of. My cofounders were recommended to me by mutual acquaintances who were somehow able to discern that we would likely make a great team. Like any passionate entrepreneur, I was always sharing my work with people and was always on the lookout for people with whom I could share this journey.

Clarisse Iribagiza / DMM.HeHe

founders

What was the original goal behind founding HeHe?
Our simple goal at the start was to connect people to products and services they might be looking for around the city with ease. We wanted people to have this available at their fingertips, so mobile and geolocation technologies were and have always been central to our product design. Through several product iterations, experiments and lessons, we continue to pursue this goal and have expanded our vision to encompass digitizing supply chains across the continent.

How would you define the need that HeHe is tackling, and what makes your approach and philosophy unique?
Ultimately, we want to enable people to live life abundantly and to have access to the goods and services they need in order to achieve that goal. Our tagline is "Delivering Abundance," and we aim to do that by creating a perfect market where we can effectively match supply and demand. Digitizing supply chains is the first step in achieving that. Often, we are taught to look at life like it is a zero-sum game where the winner takes all. As a result, we tend to approach business this way. This mindset limits many businesses from forging the right kinds of relationships with their customers and other businesses, therefore limiting their growth. We adopted the abundance philosophy to guide our innovation process by always seeking to create mutually beneficial relationships with our customers and with our partners.

What were your early struggles and challenges while starting up HeHe and how did you overcome them?
My early struggles and challenges were mostly around building a great team with a collective vision and passion for what we had set out to do. I was able to overcome this by actively engaging my network to connect with like-minded people who would become my future cofounders and the rest of the team I work with today. Other challenges included having to think long-term and remain laser-focused on our vision while trying to counter the noise of short-term trends or the tendency to simply focus on the next quarter.

What do you believe was your biggest mistake, and what did you learn from it?
My biggest mistake was taking for granted the need to constantly keep growing and learning new things. I got to a point where I was not intentionally working on improving my skills and knowledge in order to deliver better results for our customers. Instead, I let the demands of my work get the better of me. So, I took a break and with the help of my husband wrote a growth plan that helped me to get out of this rut. I also joined an MBA program, and then propelled my company to the next level of growth through an acquisition.

"Our ethos is really about having an abundance mindset, completely believing that you are enough, you have enough and enough is coming in your future."

founders

What do you believe was your best decision as a founder?
My best decision as a founder was to focus on my areas of strength and partner with people who would complement me in areas that I am not necessarily good at or passionate about. I learned this from a principle called the Hedgehog Concept, created by the author of the book *Good to Great*, Jim Collins. I have since made this a required reading at the company as part of our Innovation Academy initiative. The Hedgehog Concept entails focusing on what you are passionate about and becoming the best in the world at it, so that someone is willing to pay you to do what you do. I also like to remember a quote from Rick Warren, the author of *The Purpose Driven Life*: "It's not what you do, but how much love you put into it that matters."

How have you built the right team for your vision, and what are the pillars on which you hire the right talent?
Our vision is always what comes first. We all believe in what we are doing and work collectively to achieve it. And this is how we primarily hire the right talent, by looking for people who have similar ambitions and love the work we are doing and can contribute to it. This requires every member of the team to have a high level of self-awareness and a degree of clarity of purpose. It goes back to the Hedgehog Concept I mentioned. This has been much more difficult than it sounds, and we often do not spend enough time answering these questions for ourselves, which shows how important it's been for building the right team.

Have you cultivated any personal work habits? How do you keep yourself disciplined and inspired?
I try to always make sure I am learning and growing in my areas of expertise, whether through formal education programs, networks or books. I keep myself disciplined and inspired by surrounding myself with people who know my dreams and ambitions and keep me accountable for working towards achieving them. Through the HeHe Innovation Academy, we've designed programs to keep us, me included, growing and learning.

founders

What philosophies and activities have you instilled in your team culture?
What makes your team unique?
Our ethos is really about having an abundance mindset, completely believing that you are enough, you have enough and enough is coming in your future. And we preach this through the HeHe Innovation Academy to our teams and partners.
It is an overarching philosophy not just for product innovation, but for all aspects of entrepreneurship, from team building to investor relations and so much more.

What are the biggest challenges you see ahead, and also the hopes you have moving forward?
The abundance philosophy was embraced by our team as an answer to some of the biggest challenges in our entrepreneurial ecosystem, choosing to think abundantly, or in terms of win-win scenarios, and long-term in our approach to creating innovations for the continent and beyond.

[About]   Founded in 2010, DMM.HeHe builds mobile-first geolocation technologies that support the vision of bringing Africa into the fourth industrial revolution. The company uses technology to create efficient distribution services to match supply and demand for SMEs in Africa, which allows for greater reach for the businesses and better access to goods for customers. DMM.HeHe digitizes consumer goods and distribution channels and serves over two million users across the continent.

[Links]   Web: dmmhehe.com LinkedIn: company/dmm-hehe-ltd Facebook: HeHelabs
Instagram: dmm.hehe_ltd Twitter: @DMMHeHe

Clarisse Iribagiza / DMM.HeHe

What are your top work essentials?
Internet connectivity and a quiet working environment.

At what age did you found your company?
Twenty-two.

What's your most-used app?
Google Drive closely followed by WhatsApp.

What's the most valuable piece of advice you've been given?
You were created for a purpose, so live each day in pursuit of that.

What's your greatest skill?
I'm not sure.

founders

Henri Nyakarundi

Founder and Managing Director / ARED

A serial entrepreneur with an affinity for impact-driven business, Henri Nyakarundi founded ARED with technology that applies a simple solution to a widespread problem. The evolution of his company from a tech-based startup to a B2B supplier holds lessons about building partnerships, prioritizing a sustainable business model over tech trends and being adaptable at all times.

When did you know that you were an entrepreneur at heart?
I knew a job was not for me, let me put it that way! I knew I wanted to be an entrepreneur when I started working in a sales position on commission. From there, I knew the concepts behind working for a fixed salary or being in control of your destiny. To this day I look at entrepreneurship in the same way: you're more in control of your destiny, you're in control of your revenue, and the effort you put in usually equates to what you get out. In the beginning, at least, that's what really pushed me toward entrepreneurship, and from that day I've never looked back.

Where did your success in business begin?
Trucking was my first successful business, my definition of success being that you're cash-flow positive. There was a huge gap between the time I started entrepreneurship and the time I started my first successful business – close to eight years. Trucking came about by accident, like a lot of my businesses. While I was working for Kinko's, I met a truck driver who became my good friend. I was working the third shift at night and this truck driver came in to copy his pay stub and we started a conversation. I asked him a lot of questions and from the feedback he gave me, I thought it wasn't a very hard business. It seemed like a very lucrative opportunity. But of course, the reality was not always exactly that. I started immediately, did my research, registered a company and, in two or three months, I was in the trucking business.

Henri Nyakarundi / ARED

What motivates you?

Back then, the opportunity was financial – I was always looking for businesses with high returns and little investment needed. Those were my criteria back then, and trucking was exactly that. To get a license to get a trucking company, you don't need to have trucks – you can hire truck owners to operate under your license – so the investment was very minimal, and I just wanted to plug into the industry and build a business around it. Nowadays there's a lot of innovation in trucking, but back then I was not thinking about innovation. I was just thinking about a business that I can do, that can generate a good amount of money. Remember that before my trucking business, all my businesses had failed, for different reasons. Trucking, in my mind, was my last hope. My family, at that point, was tired of financing what they called "my dreams." They gave me a talk, like, "maybe entrepreneurship is not for you." So this was my last chance, basically, and I had no room for error. And it took me a little while to make this business profitable. It took exactly two years – I remember it like it was yesterday – but I made it happen.

You're from Rwanda, but studied and started your business in the US. What brought you back to start a business in Rwanda?

ARED was born due to certain circumstances that happened in America, the first of which was the financial crash in 2008. By that time I was in trucking and I was in real estate – I had a good amount of cash flow, so I was buying houses – and overnight, all my real estate value dropped by fifty percent. I didn't get affected too much on the trucking side but my real estate was affected dramatically.

I was also starting to get news of Africa growing – the narrative was changing. I was visiting Rwanda every year on vacation and I was starting to see the changes, with Rwanda already implementing the Rwanda Development Board. All of these concepts were interesting and compelling to me, and they helped me to make the decision that it was time to move back. So I looked at different industries that I could bring value to and ended up deciding between energy and agriculture, but energy was more interesting to me than the agricultural sector.

From my personal experience in Burundi, I could see the growth of cellphones, but unfortunately people were having a huge problem charging those phones. I'd seen that you could charge your phone at airports and thought, well, it would be cool to have charging kiosks in high-traffic areas. In 2009, I put together the concept, and it took three years to develop the prototype. After the first prototype, I moved back home.

Henri Nyakarundi / ARED

"*My first advice would be to build a model that's sustainable. Don't depend on grants, don't depend on subsidies, because one day or another, when they stop, you're dead in the water.*"

founders

What brought about a move into the world of impact-driven business?
My first decade in business, my twenties, I was always focusing on money. Then, when I had my first successful business, I realized that making good money did not bring the joy that I was expecting. I mean, it helped! But I thought I was going to be fulfilled, that I was going to be much happier. But I'd come to find that trucking was not a business I liked, to be honest, and I realized that there had to be something more than just money. I started reading a lot more about impact at that time and I slowly started shifting into a more impact-focused mindset. That really helped me to mold what ARED is now. I realized that doing for others is much more fulfilling than doing for yourself.

ARED has also evolved dramatically. The initial idea of ARED was phone charging using renewable energy because access to energy was a huge problem, especially in the refugee camps where we operated. It was a good service, but it was not enough to build a sustainable business. We had to evolve and move the business to a more B2B model. We looked at what other services we could bring to better monetize our platform. How could we develop an additional model where revenue would come not from the user but from businesses, organizations and NGOs who value what we're trying to do? That's why we're now more into digital technology, using renewable or clean tech to power the solution. The majority of our revenue comes from digital services.

We built a mini-server on the kiosk that would allow us to provide offline applications like contacts, gaming, surveys and offline payments. What I mean by "offline" is that the user doesn't need the internet to interact digitally on the platform.

What are some of the biggest challenges you've faced in business?
Building an impact business is the hardest thing I've done because most of my other businesses were B2B. B2B and B2C are even more challenging to low-income people because you're dealing with a different mindset. You cannot just bring a service to low-income people and expect them to adopt it. They don't necessarily have access to technology and an understanding of it. You have to build a value chain and infrastructure partners. That's why you see that the rate of failure in that space is massive – most of those businesses are not sustainable. Most of them depend on grants or subsidies.

founders

We now have a B2B model where we provide our technology solution to businesses, so that offsets some of the loss in our impact business. That's allowed us to build a hybrid business model – "hybrid" for us means that you do an impact business, but you also look at what you can do with your technology in a traditional business that can bring much higher revenue and offset some of the loss that you generate on your impact business. You're going to generate a loss no matter how great your technology is. Because of the margins and the investment you make on infrastructure, training and more, you're going to lose some money.

What would be your advice to a young entrepreneur starting a business?
If they're an impact entrepreneur, my first advice would be to build a model that's sustainable. Don't depend on grants, don't depend on subsidies, because one day or another, when they stop, you're dead in the water. Build what I call a modular business model. Minimize the footprint on the value chain of your business. Don't try to do everything: find partners who can help you on that value chain. On the training side, in the refugee camps, we work with NGOs. On the data plan, and on the services we provide, we try to find partners on our value chain. That's going to minimize your operating expenses dramatically and maximize the potential for revenue.

On the traditional business side, focus more on your business model than on the technology itself. I used to believe that it was the technology that makes or breaks you as a business, but no. The business model is the most important part, especially in Africa. Africa is a very challenging ecosystem because of how fragmented the market is, how taxes are set up, how every country has different laws – you have to have a very, very dynamic business model that is highly modular, where you can make changes very quickly and not have a lot of footprints. We don't even set up shop in any country anymore. Instead, we work with local partners.

[About]   ARED produces a solar-powered, business-in-a-box kiosk that allows its users to charge their phones, access wifi and use an intranet with free digital content. The company leases this equipment to partner organizations operating in Rwanda and Uganda.

[Links]   Web: aredgroup.com LinkedIn: company/african-renewable-energy-distributor-ared-
Facebook: aredgroup Instagram: aredgroup Twitter: @AREDRwanda

Henri Nyakarundi / ARED

What are your top work essentials?
Partners and clients in new markets to push our expansion plan.

At what age did you found your company?
I was thirty-five when I started ARED.

What's your most-used app?
LinkedIn.

What's the most valuable piece of advice you've been given?
Never give up on your dream, no matter what.

What's your greatest skill?
Problem solving – always finding a solution to any challenge.

founders

Patrick Buchana Nsenga

Cofounder and CEO / AC Group

Patrick Buchana Nsenga cofounded AC Group with a group of friends in 2013. He also serves on the board of directors for the Private Sector Federation of the Rwandan ICT Chamber and is an Invest in Africa forum committee member. Patrick has received many awards in ICT, including the 2018 Young Rwandan Achievers Award and an Innovation Champion award from the 2014 Innovation Prize of Africa. He has also long been involved with youth activities in the ICT sector and helped initiate Tech Support Incike, a charity for survivors of the 1994 genocide.

How did the idea for AC Group come about?
AC Group was founded in 2013 and started operations in late 2014. As a student, I used public transport to commute from my residential area to the part of the city where my university was. It took twenty minutes on some days and an hour and a half on other days, even though the time and day of the week were exactly the same. It was very difficult to make plans around public transportation. Out of curiosity, I asked what caused these delays and what could be done about them. I knew that this was not just a problem for me, but for everybody – working class people, students, people who had medical appointments, everybody.

I found out that bus companies were losing a big portion of their revenue to cash handling. This was mainly revenue lost due to leakage between the driver and the conductor who collected the money. I also found out that there were big price fluctuations. For example, if it was raining, and the driver knew you had no other means of commuting, the price would skyrocket. Obviously public transportation was not a very attractive option for people who couldn't afford this sudden hike in price. We thought about innovations that were used in the rest of the world and eventually introduced the Tap&Go card.

Patrick Buchana Nsenga / AC Group

The Tap&Go card did two important things. First, it ensured price stability. Second, bus companies recovered the revenue that was lost due to leakage between the bus driver and the conductor. We learned that this leakage accounted for thirty to forty percent of lost revenue, which is quite significant. We then asked the bus companies to reinvest the recouped money into more buses to help public transport run more efficiently. As we grew, we kept on innovating and looking for ways to create an unmatched experience for commuters. Our ultimate goal is to create a product that makes public transport a more attractive option than commuting to work by car.

Could you talk a bit more about those innovations?
We are always thinking of new solutions. After introducing the Tap&Go card, we started building other solutions on top of it. In addition to the initial payment system, we added a fleet-management component. With this component you can see, for example, how far the next bus is from a stop. By using the data created over the previous period, you can also match the number of buses with the number of passengers. Bus companies can basically optimize their fleet and send buses where they are needed at the appropriate times, which ultimately reduces delays. We have also developed a second Tap&Go card product, which provides fast wireless internet onboard the buses. Commuters spend about forty-five minutes a day commuting on average and we want to make sure that their time is productive and enjoyable. Currently, we have about 300,000 people using wifi each day.

The Tap&Go solution has grown. Now all transactions on public transportation in Kigali are completely cashless. We started with the Tap&Go payment, added the fleet-management solution and then added 4G wifi. We are also helping bus companies become more creditworthy to financial institutions by providing them with accurate information on how much money they have made. We give them the ability to buy new buses and reinvest revenue into their business. They now have more cash flow, which allows them to grow.

We have also added the utilization of data, mapping the movement of buses to passenger traffic. This data has helped the Government of Rwanda build up their Public Transport Generation 2 initiative, which is smart, scheduled public transport.

"As leaders, our primary focus is getting the right team, empowering them to do their job and constantly enhancing their strengths while working with them on their weaknesses."

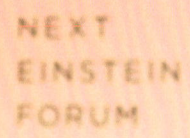

founders

Can you talk a little bit about your own entrepreneurial journey?
It started back when I was at university. Quite frankly, I never thought I would be an entrepreneur until I actually started the business. I like technology, and I was studying electronics and telecommunications. I looked at the gap that was there and thought that technology could be used to solve it. I founded the company on my technology background. I then tried to find a mentor who had been in the entrepreneurship space. I had never understood that building a business is a lot more than just providing the technology. I had to invest a lot of time learning about management and how to set up a business that is not just technologically capable but has structures that allow the business to both grow and enable a technology built to scale.

My urge to make the business succeed and my desire to build public transport that could be used by everyone gave me the energy to keep pushing myself with the parts of business I didn't like but had to learn.

Were you pretty much working alone at the beginning?
We started with a very lean team of about five people. I looked at one area where I didn't have a lot of experience – public transport – and brought in someone who was familiar with that. We had two other people who were very good at hardware installations and we had other people who could sell. It was a beautiful mesh of skills. Everybody was so good at what they did that nobody had to do too much outside their field of knowledge.

Learning the business side was a challenge. What other challenges did you have to overcome?
The first challenge was to get funding. At the beginning, we raised money in bits and pieces. We would get money and then, after three months, it would run out and we would have to look again. As a business grows, you have to spend time looking for money when you should instead be focusing on your business. That was very difficult. The second challenge was recruiting talent. We had a big vision and wanted to grow into a very big company, but we never had the resources to recruit the best talent. Instead, we hired people who were committed and whose values aligned with our own. We tried to train ourselves from the ground up to learn the skills that were needed to have a company at that scale. That was also very difficult.

founders

Can you think of one mistake you made that was bigger than the rest?
Initially, part of our system was built outside the company and we kept putting off making a firm decision to build everything in-house. It took two years to make that decision. It should have been made earlier.

What about the best decision you made in this process?
The best decision we made in this process was to forego the profits we would have made much earlier and instead reinvest almost all of it back into the business. From the management to the shareholders, we agreed to reinvest almost everything to build for the future. This has had a big ripple effect because our growth has been exponential but also, more importantly, we have centered our growth around our core purpose. Constantly looking for funding would have caused us to forego some of the core developments and principles that have led us to where we are today.

Can you think of something that you wish you had known before?
The obvious one is to focus on the management side of the business as much as the technology. That would have made a big difference for us.

Do you have advice for other entrepreneurs?
As leaders, our primary focus is getting the right team, empowering them to do their jobs and constantly enhancing their strengths while working with them on their weaknesses. With that, you can guarantee victory over any obstacles and build a business that will grow exponentially.

What do you like about working in Kigali?
The best thing is the stakeholder relationships we have with the government and the bus companies. It's such a relief to sit down with everyone, have discussions around the future and feel like they are listening. They are truly ready to support us and change regulation in order to accommodate some of the innovation around public transport. This is something I have not seen elsewhere – not only in our region, but on the continent. Kigali is also a very beautiful place. It's very green. Also, the people are lovely and you can actually hear birds singing every morning.

[About] AC Group is a Rwandan tech company that provides smart solutions to public transport. Since its development of the Tap&Go card in 2015, it has initiated cashless payments on all buses in Kigali, introduced 4G wifi on all buses and created a fleet-management system.

[Links] Web: acgroup.rw LinkedIn: company/acgrouprwanda Instagram: acgrouprw Twitter: @acgrouprw

Patrick Buchana Nsenga / AC Group

What are your top work essentials?
My notebook, iPad and my earphones.

At what age did you found your company?
Twenty-four.

What's your most-used app?
WhatsApp.

What's the most valuable piece of advice you've been given?
Hire for values. You can do talent along the way, but not the other way around.

What's your greatest skill?
Comprehending something and trying to find a way forward.

sch

ools

African Institute for Mathematical Sciences **136**

African Management Institute **138**

Akilah Institute **140**

Moringa School **142**

University of Rwanda **144**

schools

- Be innovative.
  You should demonstrate innovation and creativity.

- Show you can lead.
  We are looking for students who can demonstrate strong leadership qualities.

- Be passionate.
  You should have a genuine passion for using mathematics for development.

- Think Pan-African.
  You should have a Pan-African spirit and a desire to develop solutions for the whole continent.

African Institute for Mathematical Sciences

[Name]

[Elevator Pitch] *"We are Africa's first and largest network of centers of excellence in mathematical sciences with focus on mathematical sciences, climate science and machine intelligence."*

[Enrollment] **Students per year: 50 per center**

[Description] Founded in South Africa in 2003 by globally acclaimed South African physicist Neil Turok, the African Institute for Mathematical Sciences (AIMS) is a network of centers of excellence in mathematical sciences, climate science and machine intelligence. It has locations in Senegal, Ghana, Cameroon and Rwanda, and is currently headquartered in Kigali. Over two thousand individuals from forty-three countries have graduated from the institution since its inception. AIMS empowers young mathematicians to shape the continent's future through a twenty-four-hour learning environment with top international and local lecturers. "The twenty-four-hour environment opens up opportunities of interaction among students, tutors and lecturers even beyond class hours," says Professor Sam Yala, AIMS Rwanda Centre president. "The Pan-African nature of the institute fosters interaction and grooming of ideas at the centers."

AIMS is also a research hub and it works to increase collaboration between the public and private sectors to prioritize STEM education, research and innovation in Africa through policy and foresight. The institute wants to improve the lab-to-market process by preparing AIMS graduates to support Africa's private sector or become "sciencepreneurs" and create their own startups. Its master's degrees in mathematical sciences include a structured ten-month program that prepares students to quickly continue on to a research master's, PhD or research-related career. AIMS also offers students a cooperative education option that includes the structured master's program plus six months working in industry to apply the skills learned to real-life challenges.

Students receive a full scholarship including tuition, room and board, travel grants to and from AIMS centers and a stipend. Funding is made possible by support from local governments, the Government of Canada, the Mastercard Foundation and others. The institute also runs the Next Einstein Forum, through which it helps African governments and businesses to fund and leverage innovation.

[Apply to] **nexteinstein.org/apply**

[Links] Web: **nexteinstein.org** LinkedIn: **company/aims---next-einstein-initiative**
Facebook: **AIMSNext** Twitter: **@AIMS_Next** Instagram: **aims_next**

schools

- **Be curious.** The most important thing we're looking for is curiosity, and tied into that is an intrinsic motivation to learn.

- **Have internet access.** It doesn't need to be an amazing high-speed connection, but reliable access is a practical requirement.

- **Be willing to experiment in the workplace.** You need to be willing to experiment and take your learning into the workplace. It's not just about learning great theory, but also about being willing to make the changes in your everyday life.

- **Be collaborative.** We place a strong emphasis on peer learning and working together on solutions. If you're willing to talk about issues, you're going to get a lot out of our programs.

African Management Institute

[Elevator Pitch] "African Management Institute enables ambitious businesses across Africa to thrive. We believe that skilled people build thriving businesses, that thriving businesses create quality jobs and that quality jobs drive prosperity and dignity."

[Enrollment] Students per year: 1,500

[Description] Founded in 2014 by Jonathan Cook, a former director of Gordon Institute of Business Science, and Rebecca Harrison, a social entrepreneur and foreign correspondent, African Management Institute (AMI) is a truly modern learning organization. Its blended approach of experiential learning and online classroom resources allows students to gain entrepreneurship skills and business savviness at their own speed and according to their particular needs. AMI runs twelve programs of varying lengths and skill levels, including a management training institute for larger companies, business-development-support programs for SMEs and a youth leadership program. Its Survive to Thrive program is aimed at helping small businesses affected by major disruptions in their markets. The programs are low-cost or fully sponsored by a third party, and the technology-forward approach makes them accessible to both early-stage entrepreneurs and more established companies. "They're not just learning theory outside of the workplace but, more importantly, skills to use inside the workplace," says Diederik Wokke, country manager for AMI in Rwanda. "No matter where you are in your career or in your business, you'll always be able to identify areas where you might be lagging behind and our programs can help you improve."

AMI's teaching model is based on best-in-class research on adult learning: 70 percent hands-on experience, 20 percent learning skills and 10 percent theory. Examples of hands-on learning include picking up bookkeeping or developing customer service skills. Typically, entrepreneurs who take part in the program meet for an in-person orientation and then continue to learn through an online platform as they build their business, but the COVID-19 pandemic caused the program to adapt and go fully online. Diederik says, "A real advantage is that we had a lot of experience before this all started. It was quite an easy shift, because it was not like we needed to go from full classroom model to an online model. That helped us to pivot very quickly."

[Apply to] Diederik Wokke, diederik@africanmanagers.org

[Links] Web: **africanmanagers.org** LinkedIn: **company/african-management-institute**
Facebook: **africanmanagers** Instagram: **african_managers** Twitter: **@africamanager**

schools

- Be a changemaker.
  Students should demonstrate the vision and drive to create positive change in their communities.

- Be open-minded.
  You should be able to question your assumptions and be ready to challenge the status quo.

- Demonstrate hunger.
  You need to be hungry and passionate about acquiring knowledge and skills.

- Be an ethical leader.
  You should have a desire to become part of a community of thoughtful leaders committed to building the future with respect.

- Be focused on sustainability.
  We believe that a sustainable mindset is a career competency and we want students to learn to balance vibrant economies with a healthy environment.

[Name] # Akilah Institute

[Elevator Pitch] *"As the campus for female students at Davis College, we educate future leaders to champion opportunity and sustainability in solving the world's most pressing challenges."*

[Enrollment] **Total enrollment: 1,000 (2020)**

[Description] Founded in 2010, the Akilah Institute set out to educate the next generation of female leaders and entrepreneurs. The organization has since expanded to become Davis College, which offers leadership and entrepreneurial education to young men as well, with the Akilah Institute becoming the women's campus at the college. Aline Kabanda, president of Davis College, says that the school has ambitious plans for the next ten years. "We will impact one million students across Africa and Asia by 2030 through our competency-based blended and online diplomas and degrees," she says.

The Akilah Institute works with private sector partners to create its curricula and offers accredited diplomas in business, entrepreneurship, hospitality and tourism management, and information systems. Equipped with the skills necessary for professional success in the twenty-first century, its graduates go on to careers in finance, technology, eco-tourism and conservation, among other sectors. Eighty-six percent of graduates launch their careers within six months of graduation, and on average they earn eleven times the national median income. "Rather than just completing credit hours, our outcomes-based, student-centered approach to learning means students prove mastery of specific competencies before advancing to the next level, focusing on what they know and can do," says Aline.

The school has launched an innovative tech platform to match graduates with careers, and it leverages adaptive learning tools within its courses. It also provides extensive supplementary training in soft skills such as leadership development, career preparation and English-language communication. Its flagship course is its Business Management and Entrepreneurship diploma, which exposes students to core elements of establishing and maintaining a business, such as marketing and management, while also sharpening their skills in innovation and creativity.
"The successful outcome of our diploma is an all-round graduate who has the necessary knowledge, skills and disposition to handle the rigors of the current and future business environment," says Aline.

[Apply to] akilahinstitute.org

[Links] Web: akilahinstitute.org LinkedIn: school/akilah-institute-for-women Facebook: akilahinstitute Instagram: akilahinstitute Twitter: @AkilahInstitute

schools

- Demonstrate aptitude.
  Applicants should have knowledge of mathematics or statistics, and a background in computer studies is an advantage.

- Show your passion.
  Successful programmers need to be passionate about all things tech and innovation.

- Focus on the future.
  You should have a deep desire to acquire the practical skills needed for a career in tech.

- Be willing to learn in a different way.
  We are looking for students passionate about learning and comfortable with both face-to-face and virtual lessons.

Moringa School

[Name]

[Elevator Pitch] *"We provide transformative, tech-based learning experiences through an industry-specific curriculum, practical experience and a blended learning approach that allies tech-skills development with life-skills education."*

[Enrollment] **Students per cohort: 90**

[Description] Founded in Kenya in 2014 by Audrey Cheng, Moringa School's mission is to transform higher education throughout Africa and enable its graduates to be globally competitive. Its curriculum consists of pre-prep, prep and core modules for software development and data science. The school provides experienced trainers and mentors, a blended learning model that combines hands-on teaching with virtual modules, and a market- and outcomes-driven curriculum to train Africa's future engineers. It has supported the placement of more than 85 percent of its graduates into leading companies throughout Africa and across the globe. Tuition fees are paid by sponsoring partners.

The Moringa School launched in Kigali in 2018, in partnership with the ICT Chamber and PSF and funded by GIZ. So far, seventy-six students from two women-only cohorts have graduated from its WeCode course, a version of the software-development program. The first of these cohorts had a job placement rate of 88 percent. "Some of the institutions where our graduates are currently employed include Irembo Gov, MobiCash, Awesomity Lab and Andela," Audrey says.

The software-development course available in Kigali requires six months of full-time learning. It features a four-week pre-prep program that aims to develop and bring students up to speed with basic coding, followed by a five-week fundamentals course that covers foundational concepts in programming using JavaScript. A final four-month course provides more in-depth training and has two tracks: full stack and Android software development. The school's curriculum is aimed at both complete beginners to programming and more established developers looking to sharpen their skills and launch careers. Moringa School plans to continue its active engagement in Rwanda while also planning further expansion. "We have offered our curriculum in other regions, including Pakistan, through partnerships with the World Bank and Pakistani government; Hong Kong, in collaboration with Accelerate; and Ghana, with Meltwater Entrepreneurial School of Technology," Audrey says.

[Apply to] moringaschool.com

[Links] Web: moringaschool.com LinkedIn: linkedin.com/school/moringa-school
Facebook: moringaschool Instagram: moringaschool Twitter: @moringaschool

schools

- Aspire to be an employer and an active member of your industry.
  We're looking for people who want to involve themselves in Rwanda's economy and make meaningful differences in the lives of others.

- Have an idea with a social or environmental impact.
  The Executive MBA in Impact Entrepreneurship is designed to support individuals who have already begun building their business, either conceptually or in reality, and we prefer ideas with impact at their core.

- Be a problem solver.
  We're looking for people who are proactive and innovative and who aim to find solutions both in their business and in society at large.

- Meet our minimum entry requirements.
  Each program has different requirements. We ask that all applicants to the Executive MBA in Impact Entrepreneurship have a bachelor's degree with honors and can demonstrate sufficient English language ability.

University of Rwanda

[Elevator Pitch] *"The University of Rwanda is a leading young university determined to produce graduates who are innovators and leaders. Its Executive MBA in Impact Entrepreneurship aims to give entrepreneurs a results-oriented education while they run their business."*

[Enrollment] Total enrollment: 10,000 (2020)

[Description] The University of Rwanda was formed through the consolidation of seven higher learning institutions to create one public entity representing Rwanda's academic ability. Since its foundation in 2013, the university has proved to be a forward-thinking and innovative institution that prepares students to engage with a global economy and academic ecosystem. It offers a wide range of programs, many of which include interdisciplinary courses in partnership with universities abroad.

One of the university's six colleges, the College of Business and Economics has four core campuses in Gikondo, Huye, Nyagatare and Rusizi. It offers both undergraduate and postgraduate programs including several MBAs and aspires to be a central pillar in the East African business community. It has a mission to engage in research and community service and promote democratic culture for the development of the country. The college's graduates form a network of entrepreneurs who embody its core values of innovation, excellence and community engagement.

The Executive MBA in Impact Entrepreneurship is offered in partnership with Milan's Università Cattolica del Sacro Cuore, from which participants receive their diploma. This unique program admits up to sixty students in each cohort and is ideal for entrepreneurs who have a concept or existing business to which they can apply their education in real time. It is taught using a blended learning method with intensive weeks of in-class lessons as well as distance learning. Throughout the program, students have a dedicated business coach who provides individual support. Over fifteen months, students move through three key phases, each including a boot camp component and a competition. The program allows students to learn concepts such as strategizing, problem solving and scaling and apply them to their individual enterprises.

[Apply to] admissions.ur.ac.rw

[Links] Web: **ur.ac.rw** LinkedIn: **school/university-of-rwanda** Facebook: **UniversityofRwanda** Twitter: **@Uni_Rwanda**

inve

stors

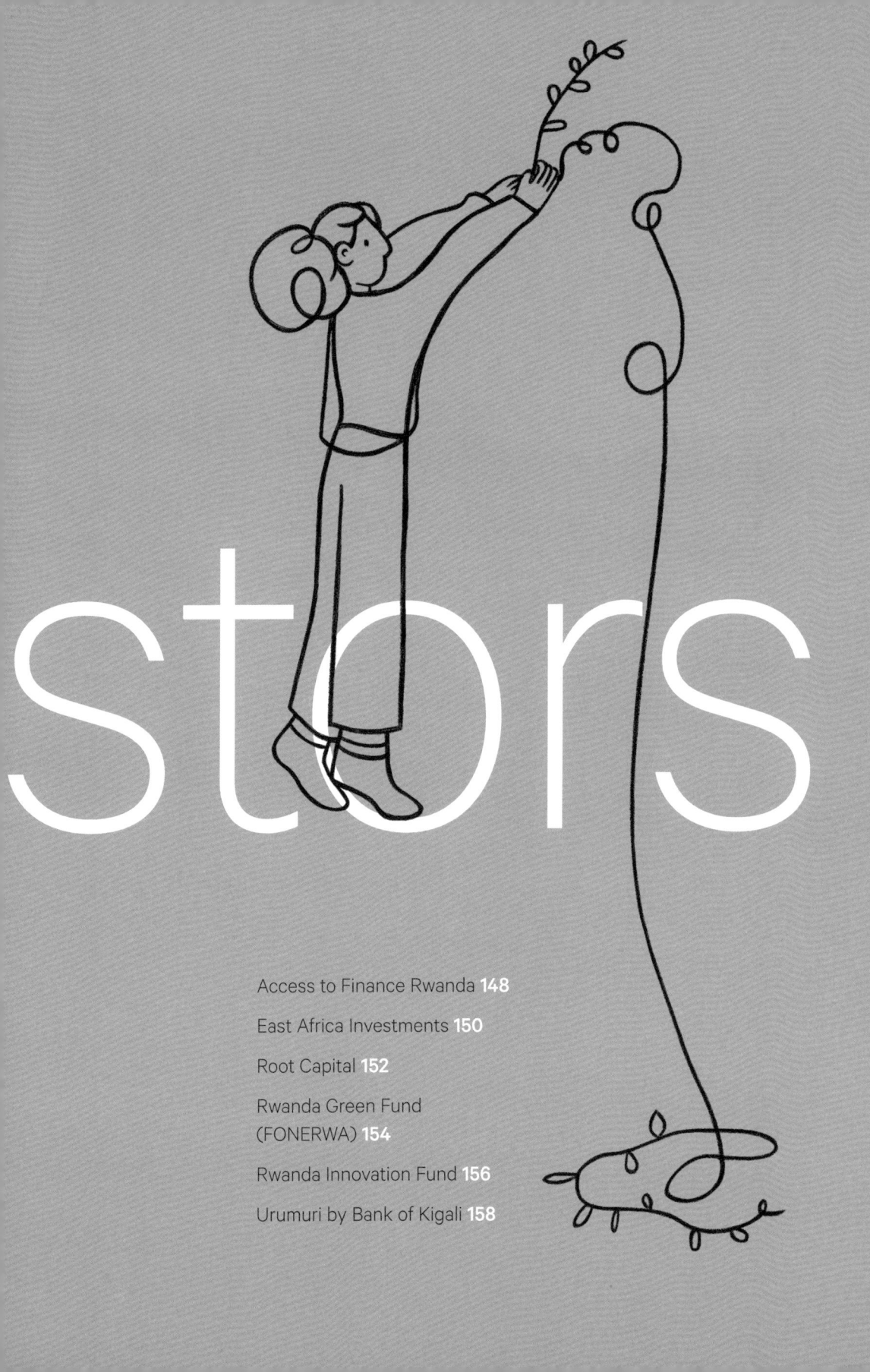

Access to Finance Rwanda **148**

East Africa Investments **150**

Root Capital **152**

Rwanda Green Fund (FONERWA) **154**

Rwanda Innovation Fund **156**

Urumuri by Bank of Kigali **158**

investors

- Have an innovative solution.
  We are looking for projects that address financial services in creative and unique ways.

- Address a real need.
  There should be a focus on impact, whether that is social, economic or environmental. How does your project support people?

- Indicate a high potential for growth.
  We are interested in startups that are able to expand to new markets and fields.

- Be scalable.
  We love to invest in startups that can expand beyond the immediate community affected, either to new regions or even new countries.

- Be sustainable.
  Your project or startup should have a long shelf life, meaning that it can show the potential to be replicated and expanded in a sustainable way.

[Name] # Access to Finance Rwanda

[Elevator Pitch] *"We promote financial inclusion and financial-sector development in Rwanda for individuals, households and SMEs. Our goal is to remove the systemic barriers that hinder access to financial services by putting low-income people at the center of our interventions."*

[Sector] **Finance**

[Description] After working in commercial banking for more than seven years, Jean Bosco Iyacu, now the director of programs at Access to Finance Rwanda (AFR), felt that something was missing. Instead of focusing on turning a profit – often for individuals or institutions that didn't necessarily need the money to survive – he wanted to support his fellow Rwandans in a more hands-on and direct way. "At some point with all those years in commercial banking, I felt like we were more or less using our heads, not our hearts," he says.

Jean moved into impact investment and joined AFR in 2014. Founded in 2010, AFR uses a partnership model that brings together local lending institutions and international donors to support inclusive finance schemes aimed at low-income households. Its core objective is to stimulate the development of the financial sector in Rwanda and remove the systemic barriers that hinder access to financial services. Initially funded through the UK's Department for International Development (DFID) and the World Bank in partnership with the Government of Rwanda and the German Development Bank, it is now funded by DFID, the Mastercard Foundation, the Government of Sweden and the US Agency for International Development, and has a number of public and private sector partners. AFR's services include providing grant funding to startups and educating Rwandans in financial literacy. The organization has supported more than two million people since its inception.

For startups including online savings-group platform Mvend, AFR has helped turn a good idea into a sustainable business model that will help them attract additional outside investment. Jean says that the idea is to be more than just an investor. "Startups have multiple needs," he says. "It's not just financing; they need some business-management skills, they need to get legal advice to structure their business and partnerships properly, they need some leadership skills."

[Apply to] info@afr.rw

[Links] Web: afr.rw   LinkedIn: company/access-to-finance-rwanda   Facebook: afr.rw   Twitter: @AFRwanda

investors

- Be able to explain how your business makes money.
  By the end of your pitch, it should be clear what you are selling and who's going to pay for it.

- Have the potential to scale.
  There's a difference between something that will grow to be an owner-operated business, like a hair salon, versus something that is genuinely scalable, like a fintech company.

- Make a return on investment.
  There's a real challenge in Rwanda because an entire generation has grown up only experiencing donor money. You've got to be able to give us the money back in three years and then some.

- Don't reinvent the wheel.
  It's ok to "copy with pride" and create a business model that has been successful in other countries, but creating a copy of something as sophisticated as YouTube for the Rwandan market is unlikely to succeed.

- Focus on impact.
  We are doing this to make a profit but we also want to make an impact.

East Africa Investments

[Name]

[Elevator Pitch] *"We are an impact investment company focused on bringing supportive capital to entrepreneurs in the East Africa region."*

[Sector] Sector-agnostic

[Description] Joanna Nicholas was a successful management consultant in the UK, but something was missing from her life – she wanted to make a bigger impact. She says that she was "tired and unhealthy" when she applied for Voluntary Service Overseas in 2006. The organization matched her with a disability nonprofit in Rwanda, where she worked as a business consultant. In this role she witnessed both the challenges and the opportunities of the Rwandan business environment. In 2017, she joined East African Investments (EAI) as country director, where she has continued to support the growth of the local ecosystem. "I really enjoy helping young entrepreneurs," she says.

Founded in 2012, EAI was started by a number of entrepreneurs who shared an MBA network and has grown to be one of the most important investment funds in the country. It typically invests $20,000–$100,000 in early-stage startups. EAI offers three levels of support to pre-seed and seed stage entrepreneurs. The first is Joanna, who as an entrepreneur in her own right works hands-on with founders, giving them support and advice in everything from assembling pitch decks to understanding tax obligations. The second is a board of experienced advisors who support the fund and also want to be actively involved with the startups by providing strategic advice and making connections. Finally, EAI partners with several European businesses interested in supporting social impact startups in Rwanda.

A number of successful startups have received support from EAI, including shoe business Uzuri K&Y Designs and Kasha, an ecommerce startup focused on women's health. While the fund is focused on impact investing, Joanna emphasizes that EAI is not a charity. "We're trying to do this like a professional investment fund," she says. "What Rwanda doesn't need is more charity. We've got to get our money back but we go about it in an extremely supportive way."

[Apply to] joanna.nicholas@eastafricainvestments.co.uk

[Links] Web: eastafricainvestments.co.uk LinkedIn: company/east-africa-investments-ltd

investors

- **Meet our loan and advisory requirements.**
  We provide loans to agricultural businesses that have an impact on smallholder farmers. Businesses must prove they've been operating for at least three years and have the accompanying financial statements, minimum annual revenues of $250,000 and strong commercial relationships with buyers.

- **Show us your value chain.**
  We want to understand the farmers you support and the number of companies buying your product.

- **Demonstrate equitable practices.**
  We look for businesses that elevate women and young people into positions of power and seek their input in decision-making processes.

- **Prove you have good relationships.**
  We value businesses that have proven relationships with domestic and international buyers.

- **Be growth oriented.**
  Our credit and capacity-building equip businesses to scale within their region or increase the services they can provide to the farmers they serve.

[Name] # Root Capital

[Elevator Pitch] *"We invest in the growth of agricultural enterprises so they can transform rural communities. We build long-term relationships and provide enterprises with the resources they need to grow, such as reliable access to financing and tailored advisory services."*

[Sector] Agriculture (coffee)

[Description] Root Capital was founded in 1999 by Willy Foote, a journalist-turned-social-entrepreneur. The firm has provided over $1.4 billion in loans to more than seven hundred businesses across Africa, southeast Asia and Latin America. It is backed by global private equity investors, including impact investors, NGOs and philanthropic organizations. Root Capital's focus is on providing rural agricultural businesses with loans of up to $1.5 million and advisory services to scale operations and solidify global value chains.

In 2010, Root Capital began working with businesses in East Africa. "All our clients have a farmer base," says James Nyambok, head of lending and general manager, East Africa. In Rwanda, the organization focuses on supporting SMEs whose end product is exported to buyers in Europe and the US, including coffee cooperatives. Root Capital works with these businesses to strengthen value chains because 70 percent of Rwandan farmers are subsistence farmers who must plan their yields in advance. If cooperatives have good relationships with buyers who agree to a quantity and price ahead of time, they can then organize their network of small and medium-scale farmers and everyone prospers. "Without that consistent way of going to the market, the farmer won't know what to grow for the next season," says James. The approach has proven successful. "With one client who has worked with Root Capital since 2014, we have seen a hundred-fold increase in their business growth," James says.

The Root Capital team attends coffee conferences across East Africa to meet with cooperatives and producers. Before lending, it evaluates the social impact of a loan, including the number of farmers and producers in the business chain. Even if an applicant doesn't meet the loan requirements, they can apply for advisory services and receive support to improve their financial and stakeholder management.

[Apply to] rootcapital.org/services

[Links] Web: rootcapital.org LinkedIn: company/root-capital Facebook: rootcapital Instagram: rootcapital Twitter: @RootCapital

investors

- **Show us you can make an impact.**
  We want to see how innovative a project is, how the technology will be applied and how it will have a positive environmental impact. Show us how jobs will be created, how CO_2 will be reduced and so on. Make a list of your project's impacts.

- **Address current environmental issues.**
  We look for projects that provide solutions to current and ongoing problems, such as drought, heavy flooding and an increase in malaria due to climate change. The more immediate the problem, the sooner we need to solve it.

- **Demonstrate value for money.**
  All proposals must go through a rigorous screening process. We want evidence that your project is worth investing in.

- **Have a coherent business plan.**
  Even the best ideas can't move forward without a strong business plan in place. We look for a convincing climate rationale to your plan.

[Name] # Rwanda Green Fund (FONERWA)

[Elevator Pitch] *"We are a dynamic, independent resource facility that provides targeted financial and technical support and contributes to Rwanda's vision of becoming a low-carbon and climate-resilient economy by 2050."*

[Sector] **Environment**

[Description] Rwanda Green Fund, also known as FONERWA, provides financial and technical assistance to projects that will help Rwanda meet its goals of becoming a low-carbon and climate-resilient economy by 2050. The organization is focused on critical environmental issues such as biomass replacement, green-city development, sustainable transport, waste treatment, climate-smart agriculture, renewable energy and clean water. The fund has mobilized $200 million for more than forty projects over the past seven years. Its largest partner is the Rwandan government, with other contributions coming from bilateral and multilateral development partners, international environment and climate funds and private sector financing.

Its environmental focus is what distinguishes Rwanda Green Fund from other investors. "We look at return on investment beyond how traditional funds do it. We are looking at the impact on the land, the amount of land secured against erosion, agroforest coverage, the protection of water bodies, the level of CO_2 avoided and, of course, the creation of green jobs," says CEO Hubert Ribiziba. With more than 140,000 green jobs created, 21,000 hectares of land secured against erosion and 93,000 tons of CO_2 gas emissions avoided, the return on investment has been substantial.

The fund supports companies of all sizes via innovation grants, credit lines and project-development grants. Innovation grants are performance-based investments where private sector companies, often startups, apply for up to $300,000 and provide 25 percent match funding. The credit line is a form of cheap funding where the fund, working with Rwanda's Development Bank, provides financing at 11.45 percent, well below market rate. The private sector company must contribute 30 percent match funding. Project development grants are only available to public institutions and NGOs. Rwanda Green Fund is actively seeking to develop private sector innovation at the startup level and has initiated a series of engagements with local incubators and coworking spaces.

[Apply to] fonerwa.org/apply-page

[Links] Web: **fonerwa.org** Facebook: **RwandaGreenFund** Instagram: **rwandagreenfund** Twitter: **@GreenFundRw**

investors

- **Provide a useful, tech-enabled solution.**
  We're looking for startups that identify real problems in society and make use of technology to address them.

- **Build towards a sustainable future.**
  From distributed infrastructure in the form of solar power and community gardens to the soft infrastructure of education and medical care solutions, we're interested in innovative solutions that care for people and the planet.

- **Provide the evidence behind your ideas.**
  We invest at the early growth stage, so we simply need to see very nascent revenue that demonstrates commercial traction and proof that the tech is working.

- **Focus on solutions for African people.**
  Whether you're Africa-based or Africa-led, you should have the aim of creating a product that serves the continent's needs.

[Name] # Rwanda Innovation Fund

[Elevator Pitch] *"We are a team of global investors and entrepreneurs who are focused on solving some of Africa's most important sustainability problems by funding innovative technology-based companies."*

[Sector] Tech-agnostic

[Description] "In finance, you think you're really smart, but there are a lot of things you don't know until you're an entrepreneur yourself," says Angela Homsi, cofounder and CEO of Angaza Capital. She speaks from experience on both counts. She started her career at Goldman Sachs and later worked with Sir Ronald Cohen, the "father of social investment." This background equipped her with sharp investment skills, but cofounding solar tech company Ignite Power and growing it to provide vital resources to 1.1 million people in Africa showed her that "there's a whole other resilience you need to have as an entrepreneur."

Today, Angela uses her knowledge and experience to back entrepreneurs whose businesses will have a significant impact on their wider communities. The Rwanda Innovation Fund (RIF) is managed by Angaza Capital with the aim of investing in emerging markets where tech-enabled solutions are solving real problems. Angela uses the lessons she learned early in her career, including smart capital, maximizing strengths and finding synergies, to select the most promising startups in fintech, healthtech, agritech and smart logistics, among other tech industries. Then she helps them succeed in solving Africa and the Middle East's most critical sustainability challenges.

The RIF team comprises global investors and entrepreneurs who have launched, led, grown, pivoted and exited companies, bringing their own experience of success and struggle to the collective expertise of the organization. Their hands-on guidance, connections, assistance with strategy, operational support and cross-border growth support are combined with smart capital backed by the African Development Bank, the government of Rwanda and leading financiers. With these resources behind them, RIF's investees are well equipped to serve their communities and expand their smart solutions to an international scale.

[Apply to] angazacapital.com/the-rwanda-innovation-fund

[Links] Web: angazacapital.com/the-rwanda-innovation-fund
LinkedIn: company/angaza-capital Twitter: @AngazaCapital

investors

The Ishyo Foods team with some of the company's products.

- Have an in-depth understanding of your business and its industry.
  We're looking for startups whose founders are knowledgeable about the ecosystem, value chain and industry within which they operate.

- Have an innovative idea.
  We want ideas that are genuinely new, that aim to solve problems or fill a gap in the market. We're seeking to support businesses that will have a meaningful and major impact on their industry.

- Be open to adopting technology in your business model.
  Technology is an asset in the growth of a business, and we're looking for people who are able to adapt and utilize it to transform their business.

- Be passionate about your ideas and bold about where you want to take them.
  We're looking for future leaders of their industries: businesspeople who are able to take calculated risks and who show passion and integrity in their business practices.

[Name] # Urumuri by Bank of Kigali

[Elevator Pitch] *"As part of the Bank of Kigali's corporate social-responsibility initiatives, we use a dedicated portion of the bank's operational budget towards interventions in the form of interest-free loans, support and guidance to the best startups in Rwanda."*

[Sector] Sector-agnostic

[Description] Urumuri represents a partnership between Inkomoko Entrepreneur Development and the Bank of Kigali through the bank's corporate social responsibility projects. It provides interest-free loans to SMEs in Rwanda and also works with businesses to create strategies, assist with training and advise on best practices.

Urumuri's main aim is to aid youth-led startups and help the continued development of Rwanda's economy. Startups generally need a comprehensive track record to receive funding, but, through Urumuri, people with bright ideas but no business experience are given an opportunity to realize their concept. By helping businesses grow from the outset, Urumuri is able to provide guidance that mitigates risk and supports success. The investor has supported startups in many industries, from tech-led and ideas-based initiatives to more traditional businesses that meet a gap in the market. An example is House of Tayo, which started making bow ties and grew to become a bespoke suit shop with a brick-and-mortar location as well as an ecommerce platform. An Urumuri loan allowed the company to scale and employ more people, from tailors to accountants, and to accept various forms of digital payment. Ishyo Foods, which produces jam from local fruits, is another success story.

Urumuri selects which startups to support through a competitive format. When it launched in 2017, it received four hundred applicants, of which only thirteen were chosen for consideration. Selected companies go through a boot camp of sorts, where they are coached on how to pitch and present their business to investors, before winning candidates are assigned interest-free loans and individual support.

[Apply to] bk.rw/urumuri

[Links] Web: **bk.rw/urumuri** LinkedIn: **company/bank-of-kigali-limited**
Facebook: **BankofKigali** Instagram: **bankofkigali.co** Twitter: **@BankofKigali**

directory

The following selection is a brief choice of organizations, companies and contacts available in Kigali

Startups

Awesomity Lab
KG 625 St.
Kigali
awesomity.rw

BAG Innovation
Plot 2 KG 5 Ave.
Kigali
baginnovation.rw

BeneFactors Ltd.
4th Floor, Fairview Building
KG 622 St.
Kigali
benefactors.io

Charis UAS
11 KN 14 Ave.
Kigali
charisuas.com

Exuus
KG 578 St.
Kigali
exuus.com

Imagine We
KG 550 St.
Kigali
imaginewe.rw

Kasha
Soras Towers
KN 67 St.
Kigali
kasha.co

My Green Home
Westerwelle Startup Haus
Fairview Building
KG 622 St.
Kigali
mygreenhome.rw

Rwanda Biosolution Ltd.
Gitega
Nyarugenge, Kigali
facebook.com/
rwandabiosolution

Programs

250STARTUPS
1st Floor, Telecom House
8 KG 7 Ave.
Kigali
250.rw

BPN Rwanda
PO Box 7083
6 KG 684 St.
Kigali
bpn.rw

Challenges Rwanda
Westerwelle Startup Haus
Fairview Building
KG 622 St.
Kigali
thechallengesgroup.com

Digital Opportunity Trust Rwanda
PO Box 5182
5 KG 178 St.
Kigali
rwanda.dotrust.org

G5 Business Makers Program
KG 224 St.
Kigali
g5businessmakersprogram.com

Hanga Ahazaza
Mastercard Foundation
Rwanda Office
4th Floor, Kigali Heights
KG 7 Ave.
Kigali
mastercardfdn.org/all/
hanga-ahazaza

Inkomoko Entrepreneur Development
1st Floor, Fairview Building
KG 622 Ave.
Kigali
inkomoko.com

Resonate
28 KG 674 St.
Kigali
resonateworkshops.org

Spaces

FabLab Rwanda
8 KG 7 Ave.
Kigali
fablab.rw

Impact Hub
3rd and 4th Floors, The Office
34 KN 41 St.
Kigali
kigali.impacthub.net

kLab
6th Floor, Telecom House
8 KG 7 Ave.
Kigali
klab.rw

WAKA
KN 72 St.
Kigali
wakaglobal.com

Westerwelle Startup Haus Kigali
4th and 5th Floors, Fairview Building
KG 622 St.
Kigali
kigali.westerwelle.haus

Experts

SAP
4th Floor, Cavendish Building
14 Riverside Park
Riverside Dr.
Nairobi
Kenya
sap.com/africa

Segal Family Foundation
13 KG 5 Ave.
Kimihurura, Kigali
segalfamilyfoundation.org

directory

Some of the websites in the Directory require the 'www' prefix.

Founders

AC Group Ltd.
99 KG 9 Ave.
Kigali
acgroup.rw

ARED Group
KN 3 Rd.
Kigali
aredgroup.com

DMM.HeHe
4th Floor, Kigali Heights Complex
K 7 Ave.
Kigali
dmmhehe.com

Water Access Rwanda
157 KN 2 Ave
BP 2376
Kigali
warwanda.com

Schools

African Management Institute
Westerwelle Startup Haus
4th Floor, Fairview Building
KG 622 St.
Kigali
africanmanagers.org

AIMS Rwanda Centre
KN 3 Rd.
Kigali
nexteinstein.org

Akilah Institute
Davis College
KN 77 Ave.
Kigali
akilahinstitute.org

Moringa School
7th Floor, Career Center Building
KG 541 St.
Kigali
moringaschool.com

University of Rwanda
PO Box 4285
KK 737 St.
Kigali
ur.ac.rw

Investors

Access to Finance Rwanda
13 KG 5 Ave.
PO Box 1599
Kigali
afr.rw

East Africa Investments Ltd.
3 Castle Hill Ave.
Berkhamsted HP4 1HJ
UK
eastafricainvestments.co.uk

Root Capital
The Arch Place
Nyangumi Rd.
Kilimani, Nairobi
Kenya
rootcapital.org

Rwanda Green Fund (FONERWA)
Career Centre Building
KG 541 St.
Kigali
fonerwa.org

Rwanda Innovation Fund
17 KG 5 Ave.
Kigali
angazacapital.com/the-rwanda-innovation-fund

Urumuri by Bank of Kigali
Plot 790
12 KN 4 Ave.
Kigali
bk.rw/urumuri

Accommodation

Airbnb
airbnb.com/kigali-rwanda/stays

Bongalo
bongalo.co

Homeland Real Estate
homeland.rw

House in Rwanda
houseinrwanda.com

Jumia
deals.jumia.rw/kigali-city/apartment-for-rent

Knight Frank
knightfrank.rw

Vibe House
vibehouse.rw

Banks

Access Bank
rwanda.accessbankplc.com

Bank of Kigali
bk.rw

BPR
bpr.rw

Cogebank
cogebanque.co.rw

Ecobank
ecobank.com

Equity Bank
rw.equitybankgroup.com

I&M bank
imbank.com/rwanda

KCB
rw.kcbgroup.com

National Bank of Rwanda
bnr.rw

directory

Coffee Shops and Places with Wifi

Bourbon Coffee
Various locations
bourboncoffee.rw

Brioche
Various locations
briocheafrica.com

BWoK
KG 383 St.
Kigali
facebook.com/bwokcafebistro

Camellia Cafe
Various locations
camelliarw.com

IINZORA Rooftop Cafe IKIREZI bookshop
13 KG 5 Ave.
Kigali
inzoracafe.com

Java House
Various locations
javahouseafrica.com

Kigali Art Cafe
KG 2 Ave.
Kigali
facebook.com/kigaliartcafe

Magda Cafe
KG 542 St.
Kigali
facebook.com/Magdacafekigali

Pure Africa Coffeebar
1 KG 676 St.
Kigali
pure-africa.com

Question Coffee
KG 8 Ave.
Kigali
questioncoffee.com

The Women's Bakery
13 KG 176 St.
Kigali
womensbakery.com

Groups and Meetups

Africa International Club
aicrw.com

Expat Entrepreneurs
facebook.com/groups/149062645773411

Expats in Rwanda
facebook.com/groups/ExpatsinRwanda

InterNations Kigali
internations.org/kigali-expats

Kigali Hash House Harriers
facebook.com/groups/kigalihash

Living in Kigali
facebook.com/groups/218647351983360

Useful Resources

American Chamber of Commerce in Rwanda
amchamrwanda.com

European Business Chamber Rwanda
facebook.com/ebcrwanda.org

Living in Kigali
livinginkigali.com

Financial Services

Bravia
KG 9 Ave.
Kigali

Dahabshiil
KN 2 Roundabout
Kigali
dahabshiil.com

PWC
35 KG 7 Ave.
Kigali
pwc.com/rw

Rwanda Stock Exchange
KN81 St.
Kigali
rse.rw

Unimoni
KG 221 St.
Kigali
unimoni.com/rwa

Important Government Offices

City of Kigali
8 KN 3 Ave.
Kigali
kigalicity.gov.rw

Irembo
KG 8 Ave.
Kigali
irembo.gov.rw

Ministry of ICT and Innovation
KN 3 Rd.
Kigali
minict.gov.rw

Rwanda Development Board
KN 5 Rd.
KG 9 Ave.
Kigali
rdb.rw

Rwanda Directorate General of Immigration and Emigration
KG 7 Ave.
Kigali
migration.gov.rw

Rwanda Finance Ltd.
KN 67 St.
Kigali
rfl.rw

Rwanda Governance Board
KG 178 St.
Kigali
rgb.rw

Rwanda Revenue Authority
KG 1 Roundabout
Kigali
rra.gov.rw

Insurance Companies

Britam
rw.britam.com

MUA Insurance
phoenix-assurance.com

Prime insurance
prime.rw

Radiant Insurance
radiant.co.rw

Sanlam
rw.sanlam.com

Language Schools

British Council
81 KG 5 Ave.
Kigali
britishcouncil.rw

Goethe Institut
2 KN 27 St.
Kigali
goethe.de/ins/rw/en/index.html

Institut Francais
KN 8 Ave.
Kigali
if-rwanda.org

Kinyarwanda Master Class
Root House
KG 548 St.
Kigali
facebook.com/kinyarwandamasterclass

Spark English
KG 622 St.
Kigali
sparkenglish.rw

Startup Events

Founders' Friday Kigali
twitter.com/FoundersKGL

Green Drinks
greendrinks.org/Kigali

Kigali Tech Happy Hour
facebook.com/kigalitech

Rwanda Fintech Forum
rwandafintech.org

Startup Grind Kigali
startupgrind.com/kigali

Twumve Twumve
globalshapers.org/hubs/kigali-hub

glossary

A

Accelerator
An organization or program that offers advice and resources to help small businesses grow

AI (Artificial Intelligence)
The simulation of human intelligence by computer systems; machines that are able to perform tasks normally carried out by humans

Angel Investment
Outside funding with shared ownership equity typically made possible by an affluent individual who provides a startup with starting capital

[see also: Business Angel]

API (Application programming interface)
An interface or communication protocol between a client and a server that simplifies the building of client-side software

B

**B2B
(Business-to-Business)**
The exchange of services, information and/or products from a business to a business

**B2C
(Business-to-Consumer)**
The exchange of services, information and/or products from a business to a consumer

Blockchain
A digital, public collection of financial accounts in which transactions made in bitcoin or another cryptocurrency are recorded chronologically

Bootstrapping
To self-fund, without outside investment

C

CAPEX
Capital expenditure; the cost of developing or providing non-consumable parts for a product or system

CEO (Chief Executive Officer)
The highest-ranking person in a company, responsible for taking on managerial decisions

Circular Economy
An economic system aimed at eliminating waste by sharing, leasing, reusing, repairing, refurbishing and recycling existing materials and products for as long as possible

**COO
(Chief Operating Officer)**
A high-level executive running the operations of a company

Coworking Space
A shared working environment

E

Early-Stage
The stage in which financing is provided by a venture capital firm to a company after the seed round; a company stage in which a product or service is still in development but not on the market yet

Elevator Pitch
A short description of an idea, product or company that explains the concept

Exit
A way to transition the ownership of a company to another company

F

Fintech
Financial technology; a technology or innovation that aims to compete with traditional financial methods in the delivery of financial services

Flex Desk
A shared desk available for temporary use in a coworking space

I

Incubator
A facility established to nurture young startup firms during their first few months or years of development

L

Later-Stage
The stage in which companies have typically demonstrated viability as a going concern and have a product with a strong market presence

Lean
Lean startup methodology; the method proposed by Eric Ries in his book on developing businesses and startups through product-development cycles

glossary

M

**MVP
(minimum viable product)**
A product with just enough features to satisfy early customers who can provide feedback for future product development

O

OPEX
Operating expenditure; the ongoing cost of running a business

P

Pitch
An opportunity to introduce a business idea in a limited amount of time to potential investors, often using a presentation

Pivot
The process when a company quickly changes direction after previously targeting a different market segment

S

SDGs (Sustainable Development Goals)
A United Nations agenda that covers seventeen global goals that can be achieved by reaching 169 defined targets

[see also: UN Goals for Sustainable Development and Sustainable Development]

Seed Funding
The first round of venture capital funding (typically called the seed round); a small, early-stage investment from family members, friends, banks or an investor, also known as a seed investor

Series A/B/C/D
The subsequent funding rounds that come after the seed stage and aim to raise further capital (up to $1 million) when the company demonstrates various increase factors

SMEs
Small and medium-sized enterprises

Social Entrepreneur
A person who establishes an enterprise with the aim of solving social problems and/or effecting social change

Startup
Companies under three years old that are in the growth stage and starting to become profitable (if not already)

Subsistence Farming
When a farmer grows food crops to meet their and their family's needs, with little to no surplus for sale

Sustainable Development
Defined by the UN World Commission on Environment and Development as an organizing principle that "meets the needs of the present without compromising the ability of future generations to meet their own needs."

U

UN Goals for Sustainable Development (SDG)
Seventeen intergovernmental development goals established by all 193 members of the United Nations in 2015 for the year 2030. The SDGs' non-binding targets provide a framework for organizations and businesses to think about and begin addressing the world's most important challenges

[see also: SDGs and Sustainable Development]

USSD
Unstructured Supplementary Service Data, a communications protocol used by cell phones to communicate with the mobile network operator or another organization's computers

UX (User experience design)
The process of designing and improving user satisfaction with products so that they are useful, easy to use and pleasurable to interact with

V

VC (Venture Capital)
A form of financing that comes from a pool of investors in a venture capital firm in return for equity

about the guide

Startup Guide Johannesburg — The Entrepreneur's Handbook
Startup Guide Hamburg — The Entrepreneur's Handbook
Startup Guide Amsterdam — The Entrepreneur's Handbook
Startup Guide Cape Town — The Entrepreneur's Handbook
Startup Guide Luxembourg — The Entrepreneur's Handbook
Startup Guide Vienna — The Entrepreneur's Handbook
Startup Guide Tel Aviv — The Entrepreneur's Handbook
Startup Guide Madrid — The Entrepreneur's Handbook
Startup Guide Copenhagen — The Entrepreneur's Handbook
Startup Guide Japan (Impact Guide Series) — The Entrepreneur's Handbook
Startup Guide Paris — The Entrepreneur's Handbook
Startup Guide Los Angeles — The Entrepreneur's Handbook
Startup Guide Reykjavik — The Entrepreneur's Handbook
Startup Guide Stockholm — The Entrepreneur's Handbook
Startup Guide Munich — The Entrepreneur's Handbook
Startup Guide Frankfurt — The Entrepreneur's Handbook
Startup Guide Zurich — The Entrepreneur's Handbook
Startup Guide London — The Entrepreneur's Handbook
Startup Guide Tokyo — The Entrepreneur's Handbook
Startup Guide Lisbon — The Entrepreneur's Handbook
Startup Guide Switzerland (Impact Guide Series) — The Entrepreneur's Handbook
Startup Guide Singapore — The Entrepreneur's Handbook
Startup Guide New York — The Entrepreneur's Handbook
Startup Guide Cairo — The Entrepreneur's Handbook
Startup Guide Bangkok — The Entrepreneur's Handbook
Startup Guide Berlin — The Entrepreneur's Handbook
Startup Guide Lagos (Impact Guide Series) — The Entrepreneur's Handbook
Startup Guide Accra (Impact Guide Series) — The Entrepreneur's Handbook
Startup Guide Nairobi (Impact Guide Series) — The Entrepreneur's Handbook
Startup Guide Kigali (Impact Guide Series) — The Entrepreneur's Handbook

startupguide.com   Follow us: @StartupGuideHQ

About the Guide

Based on traditional guidebooks and stocked with information you might need to know about starting your next business adventure, Startup Guide books help you navigate and connect with different startup scenes across the globe. Each book is packed with exciting stories of entrepreneurship, insightful interviews with local experts and useful tips and tricks. To date, Startup Guide has featured over forty cities and regions in Europe, Asia, the US, Africa and the Middle East, including Berlin, London, Singapore, New York, Cape Town and Tel Aviv.

How we make the books:
To ensure an accurate and trustworthy guide every time, we team up with local partners that are established in their respective startup scene. We then ask the local community to nominate startups, coworking spaces, founders, schools, investors, incubators and established businesses to be featured through an online submission form. Based on the results, these submissions are narrowed down to the top one hundred organizations and individuals. Next, the local advisory board – which is selected by our community partners and consists of key players in the local startup community – votes for the final selection, ensuring a balanced representation of industries and startup stories in each book.
The local community partners then work in close collaboration with our international editorial and design team to help research, organize interviews with journalists and plan photoshoots. Finally, all content is reviewed and edited and the book is designed and created by the Startup Guide team before going to print in Berlin.

Where to find us:
The easiest way to get your hands on a Startup Guide book is to order it from our online shop: startupguide.com/shop. You can also visit us at our Lisbon and Copenhagen offices:

Rua Saraiva de Carvalho 1C
1250-240 Lisbon, Portugal

lisbon@startupguide.com

Borgbjergsvej 1,
2450 Copenhagen, Denmark

copenhagen@startupguide.com

Want to become a stockist or suggest a store?
Get in touch here: sales@gestalten.com

about the guide

The Startup Guide Website

Since the first Startup Guide book was published, our network has grown and the possibilities to reach new audiences have expanded. One of the reasons we decided to start producing content through a digital platform was to be able to take a deeper look at the cities, regions and ecosystems that our books cover. We want to make it more accessible for new entrepreneurs to understand the process of getting a startup off the ground through the stories of those who were once in their shoes. By sharing educational content and inspiring examples from the startup community, our website provides valuable insights and continues our core purpose: to guide, empower and inspire people beginning their entrepreneurial path.

For more details, visit our website at startupguide.com.

#startupeverywhere

Startup Guide was founded by Sissel Hansen in 2014. As a publishing and media company, we produce guidebooks and online content to help entrepreneurs navigate and connect with different startup scenes across the globe. As the world of work changes, our mission stays the same: to guide, empower and inspire people to start their own business anywhere. To get your hands on one of our books, feel free to visit us at our offices in Lisbon and Copenhagen.

Want to learn more, become a partner or just say hello?

Send us an email at info@startupguide.com

Follow us: @StartupGuideHQ
Join us and #startupeverywhere

Kigali Advisory Board

Cares Manzi
Project Manager
and Community Lead
Impact Hub Kigali

Christian Kitumaini
Founder and CEO
G5 Business Makers
Program

Gabriel Ekman
Cofounder and CEO
BAG Innovation

Gaspard Twagirayezu
Policy Analyst
National Council for
Science and Technology

Joanna Louise Nicholas
Country Manager
East Africa Investments

Jovani Ntabgoba
Tech Investment Advisor
JICA-ICT Innovation
Project

Junior Bicura Kanamugire
Managing Director
PikiWash Ltd.

Kwena Mabotja
Regional Director,
Purpose and Brand
Experience
SAP

Liana Nzabampema
Senior Program Officer
Segal Family Foundation

Linda Mukangoga
Founder
CollectiveRW and Haute
Baso

Lionel Mpfizi
CEO
Awesomity Lab

Neil Walker
Manager
Challenges Rwanda/
Challenges Group

Norette Turimuci
Executive Director
Resonate

Olivia Bryanne Zank
Founder and CEO
BeneFactors Ltd.

Richard Rusa
Head of Product Design
DMM.HeHe Ltd.

Rob Rickard
Director
Rwanda Build Program

Sangwa Rwabuhihi
General Manager
Westerwelle Startup Haus
Kigali

Vanessa K Umutoni
Partner
Centre for Innovative
Teaching and Learning,
Mastercard Foundation –
Rwanda

Yan Kwizera
Founder and CEO
HuzaX

With thanks to our Content Partner

Segal Family Foundation

Ambassador

G5 BUSINESS MAKERS PROGRAM

IMPACT HUB Kigali

Booster

idego

Event Partner

<norrsken>

Community Partner

WSH
WESTERWELLE
STARTUP HAUS
KIGALI

Powered by
Evonik Stiftung

WHERE NEXT?